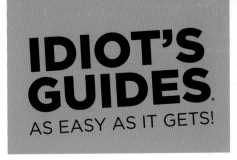

IDIOT'S
GUIDES.
AS EASY AS IT GETS!

Succulents

by Cassidy Tuttle

ALPHA

A member of Penguin Random House LLC

Publisher: Mike Sanders
Associate Publisher: Billy Fields
Executive Acquisitions Editor: Lori Cates Hand
Development Editor: Ann Barton
Cover and Book Designer: Laura Merriman

Photographer: Cassidy Tuttle
Production Editor: Jana M. Stefanciosa
Prepress Technician: Brian Massey
Proofreader: Amy Borelli
Indexer: Celia McCoy

First American Edition, 2015
Published in the United States by DK Publishing
6081 E. 82nd Street, Indianapolis, Indiana 46250

Copyright © 2015 Dorling Kindersley Limited
A Penguin Random House Company
15   16   17   18   10 9 8 7 6 5 4 3 2 1
001-280462-December2015

Published in the United States by Dorling Kindersley Limited.

IDIOT'S GUIDES and Design are trademarks of Penguin Random House LLC

ISBN: 978-1-61564-842-9
Library of Congress Catalog Card Number: 2015942373

DK books are available at special discounts when purchased in bulk for sales promotions, premiums, fund-raising, or educational use. For details, contact: DK Publishing Special Markets, 345 Hudson Street, New York, New York 10014 or SpecialSales@dk.com.

Printed and bound in China

idiotsguides.com

CONTENTS

DISCARD

INTRODUCTION

I became hooked on succulents several years ago. It seemed almost every magazine I looked at was featuring these amazing plants. Then, one of my cousins had succulents in her wedding bouquet and I knew I needed to get some. My collection started with just three plants, and soon grew to a couple hundred! I was amazed at how easy they were to take care of. I soon became interested in creating projects with these versatile plants. Since I live in a climate with cold winters, I quickly discovered that my plants would not survive outdoors after the fall. I kept as many as I could inside our small apartment. Sadly, the rest soon became victims of frost and freezing temperatures. I was determined to keep the others alive and well indoors.

GROWING SUCCULENTS INDOORS

I've discovered that it's simple and easy to grow succulents indoors. You just need to know which varieties tolerate low-light situations and the basics of caring for them, and you'll be on your way to having a great collection of plants to brighten up your space.

This book is designed to introduce you to the world of succulents. The basic principles for growing succulents indoors and outdoors are about the same. This book focuses mostly on growing indoors and includes different tips and techniques to make your indoor succulents look their best. You'll learn how to care for them and create amazing projects, as well as more about specific varieties.

SUCCULENT PROJECTS

This book includes 12 different project tutorials. They are organized with the easiest projects first and increase in difficulty. Rest assured, all of the projects can be done by anyone, and have photos to guide you every step of the way. Some of the projects are designed to be temporary, while others can last for years if they are maintained well.

CHOOSING SUCCULENTS

Our list of 100 succulents will help you decide which plants will do best for the space you have. The list features plants in a variety of shapes, sizes, and colors. While not all of the plants will do extremely well indoors, they are easy to care for. Each plant page tells the mature size of the succulent, its cold tolerance and growing zone, and its water and sun requirements, as well as a plant that will pair nicely with that species.

Growing succulents should be simple, easy, and fun. This book will help ensure you have that experience. You'll learn what you need to know to start creating your very own succulent garden in whatever space you have available!

ACKNOWLEDGMENTS

This book would not have been possible without my parents, who let me turn two of their bedrooms and a bathroom into a succulent garden, potting shed, and photo studio. Also a huge thanks to my mom, husband, and sister for being babysitters, photo assistants, and driving companions. The cute dog featured in the "Common Pests and Problems" section is Lucy, who belongs to Shaylee Linebaugh. The arrangements on pages 76–79 were photographed in the home of Meta Coleman. The long table centerpiece (pages 128–133) was photographed in the home of Sarah Champion. Also, thank you to Waterwise Botanicals and Oasis Nursery for letting me photograph in their nurseries. While most of the arrangements in the book are my own, several were created by professional succulent designers, including Jim and Desiree Castro, Katie Christensen, Cindy Davison, Mimi Hong, Adam Kopras, Erin Nielson, and Michael and Danielle Romero.

ARRANGEMENT CREDITS

Desiree Castro: 52 (right), 53 (left), 62 (right). Katie Christensen: Cover, 59 (right), 60 (left). Cindy Davison: 17, 53 (right), 58, 64 (both), 65 (right), 67 (top right), 69 (both), 71 (both), 275. Mimi Hong: 41, 63 (left), 67 (top left), 67 (bottom left), 273. Adam Kopras: 6 (left), 275. Erin Nielson: 87 (bottom), Succulent Boutonnières 146–151, Bouquet 152–157. Michael and Danielle Romero: 52 (left), 54 (right), 63 (right), 70 (both), 72 (both), 271 (right). Waterwise Botanicals: 3, 59 (left), 60 (right), 61 (bottom left), 65 (left). Oasis Nursery: 46, 47 (top).

Pottery by Susan Aach featured on pages 64 (both), 67 (top right), 69 (both), 71 (bottom), and 275 (bottom).

1

GETTING TO KNOW SUCCULENTS

You've seen succulents in magazines, on your Instagram feed, in bouquets, and in gorgeous container arrangements; they're everywhere. Maybe you're intrigued by their bright colors and unusual shapes. Maybe you've heard they're easy to take care of: "anyone can keep them alive," and "they're foolproof." Now you want some of your own, but you're not sure where to start. This section will get you headed in the right direction. There are so many things you can do with these amazing plants! You'll love deciding which plants to get and how to arrange them.

WHY ARE SUCCULENTS SO POPULAR?

More and more people are becoming interested in succulents lately, and it's no surprise! Almost anyone can find something to love about succulents, whether it's their inherent beauty, the ease of keeping them alive, their drought-tolerant nature, or their ability to propagate so effortlessly.

UNIQUE SHAPES AND STRIKING COLORS

Most people recognize succulents as rosette-shaped plants with smooth leaves and stunning colors. *Echeverias, Sedums,* and *Sempervivums* generally fit this category. They are so perfectly formed and come in a variety of stunning colors. You'll find variations of blue, purple, pink, green, orange, and red—nearly every color of the rainbow!

Once you're hooked on the rosettes, you'll discover there are many more shapes and textures of succulents you're sure to love. This variety of shape and texture also attracts many people to succulents. Succulents are being used more and more in containers, both by themselves and paired with other plants. They have clean geometric shapes that work well in modern design.

EASY TO GROW

Like all plants, it's best if you know how to care for succulents. However, you'll find succulents are pretty forgiving. For people who may not have a green thumb (and for those who do), succulents are a great place to start. Many varieties can handle quite a bit of abuse or neglect and still look gorgeous. You can find succulents to suit just about any growing conditions. For example, if you're in a small space without a lot of light, you'll find *Haworthias* and *Gasterias* will be a great fit for you.

DROUGHT TOLERANT

Succulents store water in their leaves, which makes them quite drought tolerant. You'll frequently see succulents used in waterwise gardens or even as a replacement for lawns. While they do need water, in the right environment many succulents can go weeks between watering. For those growing succulents indoors, this drought tolerance means succulents are perfect if you tend to forget to water your plants. You can leave them while you're on vacation without a worry! Many floral designers have begun using succulents in bouquets and floral arrangements because they can last several days without being watered and still look fresh.

EASY TO PROPAGATE

What's better than having one of your favorite plants? Having lots, of course! Succulents are one of the easiest plants to propagate. Many succulents will grow new babies from fallen leaves. Others grow well from cuttings, putting off new growth on the original plant and growing roots on the cutting itself. While some can be a little more complicated to propagate, many easy-to-find succulents, such as *Sedum morganianum,* propagate with almost no effort.

WHAT YOU CAN DO WITH SUCCULENTS

One of the amazing things about succulents is their ability to survive in difficult environments. They can grow in crevices between rocks by putting out roots even when there is very little soil. This makes succulents extremely fun to play with in the garden.

VERTICAL GARDENS

Succulents can grow well without much soil, and they can also grow when hanging vertically. It is becoming popular to decorate with a wall of succulents. These living pictures add a unique touch to any space. Since the succulents continue to grow, the picture constantly changes.

FLORAL ARRANGEMENTS

Succulents are becoming a popular flower choice for bouquets, boutonnières, and centerpieces because they last a long time without any water. Their perfect forms and rigid leaves provide a nice complement to softer flowers in arrangements. You can also create a temporary arrangement using only succulents, which can last for several weeks with minimal maintenance. For the same price as a bouquet of flowers, which will last only a few days, you can have a bouquet of succulents and enjoy their beauty for much longer.

UNUSUAL CONTAINERS

Since succulents don't need much soil in order to take root, you'll often see them planted in unusual containers. You can use anything that strikes your fancy, from teacups to old shoes. Succulents planted in unique containers may not last as long as they would in a standard pot because they often outgrow the space. Fortunately, you can just cut off the new growth and plant it somewhere else!

TOPIARY ARRANGEMENTS

Cuttings from succulents take root quickly, so they work perfectly for topiary arrangements. Now your succulents can grow in just about any shape or size you can imagine! As the succulents begin to grow, you'll have new plants to take cuttings from and create more topiary arrangements.

JEWELRY

You can even use succulents to decorate jewelry. With a little glue and some tiny succulents, you can create living earrings, necklaces, and more. While it won't last forever, it's sure to make a statement when you wear it.

GROWING SUCCULENTS INDOORS

Not all succulents are suited for indoor growing. In fact, there are some that won't survive well indoors at all. However, there are plenty of succulents that will grow well indoors, and even more that will tolerate it. Here are some attributes to look for when selecting a succulent to grow indoors.

TOLERANT OF LOW LIGHT

Many succulents require full sun. When you're shopping for your indoor succulent garden, be sure to choose succulents that require partial or full shade. You may even find some that prefer low light. Succulents that require full sun may grow indoors, but often they'll lose their color, shape, or both very quickly. Succulents that require shade will do quite well indoors and maintain their original form.

EXAMPLES: *Sansevieria trifasciata, Haworthia retusa*

SLOW GROWING

It is hard to know whether a succulent grows quickly or slowly just by looking at it, but with the help of the internet you should be able to find out pretty easily. The problem with keeping fast-growing succulents indoors is they tend to need more light. Without enough light they grow long and leggy. Slower-growing succulents are more likely to maintain their form. Cacti are a great example of slow-growing succulents. Often they'll prefer full sun, but because they grow slowly, they won't mind a little less light.

EXAMPLES: *Gymnocalycium mihanovichii, Mammillaria rhodantha*

NATURALLY GREEN

Succulents that have bright colors such as red or orange will often revert to green when grown indoors. Generally, succulents that are already green in color will thrive much better in lower-light settings. Plus, they won't change colors due to lack of sunlight.

EXAMPLES: *Rhipsalis cereuscula, Haworthia fasciata*

BRANCHY OR TRAILING

A succulent that naturally forms branches or grows upward is a great selection for growing indoors. Since they are already growing up, they are less likely to show signs of stretching for light. Trailing succulents also tend to do well indoors as they are also less compact. These succulents also add variety to an arrangement that may have lower-growing or compact succulents.

EXAMPLES: *Crassula ovata, Senecio rowleyanus*

If you're just starting out with succulents indoors, look for the succulents listed as examples here. They are easy to take care of and will thrive indoors. As you become more experienced with succulents or if you have a very bright room, you can begin to add others to your collection that may require more sunlight.

IDEAL SUCCULENT ENVIRONMENTS

Succulents grow in a variety of conditions, and each genera and species has its own needs. They are becoming popular for both indoor and outdoor gardens. Most succulents will do best when grown outdoors. They have better access to the light, nutrients, and air flow they need to thrive. Indoor growing spaces pose many of the same climate variations. It's best to decide where you'd like to grow succulents and pick succulents that will do best in that environment.

BRIGHT, INDIRECT LIGHT

Many succulents prefer full sun or very bright light. When grown in containers and especially indoors, most succulents will take all the light they can get, except for direct sunlight. Direct sunlight, especially in the afternoon, can easily cause succulents to sunburn or get dark spots, and can even kill the plants if it gets too hot. Try to find an area that gets morning sunlight and bright shade in the afternoon. Indoors you'll want to find somewhere that gets bright light all day.

WELL-DRAINING SOIL

The quickest way to kill a succulent is to let it sit in soggy, wet soil. All succulents appreciate a well-draining soil that allows the roots to dry off quickly. They will easily rot if left in water for too long. The next chapter includes a section about selecting the right soil for your succulents.

MODERATE TEMPERATURE

While there are succulents that can tolerate extreme heat and extreme cold, most prefer a temperate climate. A moderate temperature helps the succulent grow at its ideal rate. Too much cold or heat can damage the leaves, something that won't heal later.

AIR FLOW

Succulents need to breathe. Without proper air flow, succulents are more prone to bugs and rot. Many succulents grow in clumps and prevent air flow between the rosettes. Especially indoors, they will benefit from a little space between the rosettes. This allows the soil to dry out more quickly, which helps prevent rotting.

Although succulents need air flow, they should be kept away from indoor vents. Forced air can cause the soil to dry out too quickly, and the succulents will not have enough time to absorb the water they need.

USDA PLANT HARDINESS ZONES

Most succulents grow best outdoors in USDA Plant Hardiness Zones 9 and 10. Even within these regions, temperatures, sunlight, and water distribution can vary from house to house and in various areas of a yard.

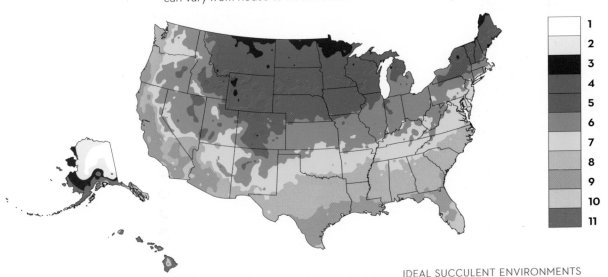

2

SUCCULENT CARE

≈≈≈≈≈≈≈≈≈≈≈≈≈≈≈≈

Succulents are great plants for beginners, but they'll survive much longer if you know how to take care of them. One of the common misconceptions about succulents is that they are hard to kill. It's true many of them can tolerate some neglect, and likely thrive better with less attention. However, many people quickly kill off their succulent collection by giving them too much love and water. This section covers the basics for growing healthy succulents. You'll also discover some of the common problems succulent growers face and how to avoid them. Soon you'll be on your way to a beautiful succulent garden!

HOW TO WATER SUCCULENTS

Watering succulents is the most important aspect of care, especially when you're first starting out. Using the right watering methods is key to keeping your succulents happy and healthy.

USE A DRAINAGE HOLE AND WELL-DRAINING SOIL

These watering instructions assume that you have a drainage hole in your pot and well-draining soil. If you don't have a drainage hole and well-draining soil, it doesn't matter how careful you are about watering; your plants will eventually die because the soil won't dry out completely. Succulents do not like to sit in wet soil, and without a drainage hole, you'll end up with wet soil around the roots that won't dry out.

A drainage hole is essential for healthy succulents.

SOAK THOROUGHLY

The arid environments where succulents naturally grow don't get rain very often, but when it does rain, it pours. Keep this in mind when watering your succulents. When you water succulents in containers, pour water on the arrangement in a slow, steady stream until the soil is fully saturated and water begins to flow out the bottom (this is why a drainage hole is so important). This will provide plenty of water for the roots to absorb.

Provide water until it begins to flow out of the drainage hol

ALLOW TO DRY

After soaking, allow the soil to dry out. When the soil has been dry for a couple days, give the succulents another soak. Having plenty of water allows the succulents to put out strong roots and soak up a lot of water to fill the leaves. They continue to grow during the period of "drought" with the water they've stored. When watered again, the plant knows it's going to be a while before more water comes and soaks up as much as it can. This is a healthy cycle that keeps the roots and plant plump and healthy.

WHERE TO WATER

A tight succulent arrangement can be difficult to water without getting too much water on the leaves. Watering the rosette of a succulent should be avoided if possible. Often water will pool in crevices on or around the leaves and cause the leaf to rot. Standing water also invites bugs to make a home in your plant. Whenever possible, water the soil around the succulent, not on top of the plant. If possible, find a watering can with a small spout. Use this to water between your plants rather than on top of them.

You can also place a watering stone in each of your arrangements. A watering stone can be any rock you like. Simply pour water on the stone and let it run off onto other areas of the container. Using a watering stone also prevents the soil or top dressing from being disturbed during watering.

A small spout can fit between plants.

misting

Many people suggest misting succulents with water. While this works on a short-term basis, it doesn't promote good root growth. Misting can work well to keep a temporary arrangement looking fresh longer, but isn't recommended for arrangements you intend to keep a long time.

Watering stones provide a spot to water.

WHEN TO WATER SUCCULENTS

While succulents are known for being drought tolerant, there is a wide range of water needs within the group. It may take some time for you to refine your watering schedule.

LET THE LEAVES BE YOUR GUIDE

As a general rule, succulents with thinner leaves will need to be watered more frequently, while succulents with thicker leaves can go longer between waterings. Along with that, succulents with thicker leaves don't tolerate overwatering as well as thinner-leaved succulents. *Echeverias* tend to be especially sensitive to overwatering.

WHEN IN DOUBT, DON'T WATER

If you're worried about how frequently you are watering your succulents, err on the side of under-watering. It is much easier to give a plant more water than to save a plant that has rotted from overwatering. Especially when growing indoors, it can be hard to know how often to water. If you're watering more than once a week and your plant isn't looking good, cut back on watering. It does take some trial and error to get on a regular schedule. Most people tend to overwater and aren't able to save their plants by the time they realize their mistake.

When leaves begin to look dry and shriveled, it's time to water.

Don't water if the soil is still wet. Err on the side of under-watering.

Plant succulents together that have the same active growing season.

PAY ATTENTION TO THE SEASON

Succulents go through a period of dormancy during which they stop growing or their growing slows down considerably. During dormancy they don't need much water. While in their active growing season, however, they like to be watered regularly. They will offset more readily, produce better colors, and look better overall if given enough water during their growing season.

Growing indoors can disrupt the dormancy cycle as there isn't a significant change in temperature or duration of light like there is between summer and winter outdoors. You'll still notice a change in the amount of growth, but it won't be as apparent. Many succulents are dormant during the winter. If you are constantly running the heater, they will dry out more quickly and will still likely need to be watered regularly.

summer growers	*winter growers*		
Agave	Aeonium	Graptopetalum	Peperomia
Ceropegia	Aloe	Graptoveria	Portulacaria
Echeveria	Cotyledon	Haworthia	Sansevieria
Euphorbia	Crassula	Kalanchoe	Sedum
Lithops	Gasteria	Pachyveria	Senecio

IDENTIFYING WATERING PROBLEMS

Overwatering is much more common than not watering enough, but both can be problematic for your plants. Here's what to look for if you suspect your succulent is getting too much water or not enough.

TOO MUCH WATER

The early signs and symptoms of overwatering can be difficult to distinguish from under-watering. One of the first signs is soft, wrinkled leaves; they'll feel similar to your fingers or toes after they've been in water too long. You'll also notice that the leaves fall off easily. The leaves are too full of water to stay properly attached.

As the damage from overwatering progresses, the lower stem of the plant and even lower leaves will start to blacken from rot. This is the easiest way to tell whether you've been overwatering, but it's hard to save your plant at this point.

To save a succulent that has been overwatered, cut off any part of the plant that hasn't been affected by the rot. If there is any black inside the stem, keep cutting it off. You don't want any black left on the cutting. Follow the directions for propagating cuttings (in the "Propagating Succulents" section) to plant the cutting.

signs of overwatering

- Soft, wrinkled leaves
- Black rot on lower stems
- Leaves fall off easily

Blackened stems are a sign of overwatering.

NOT ENOUGH WATER

Under-watered leaves tend to feel dry and almost crispy. If it has been a few weeks since you watered and your succulent is starting to shrivel, it's likely that your plant is under-watered.

When you check to see whether your plant needs water, feel the top leaves or new growth. These should feel plump and firm when properly watered. It is completely normal for lower leaves on succulents to shrivel and die after a time. This is one of the most common concerns people have with their succulents. Stores often keep their succulents cleaned up so you don't see any dead leaves. After a few weeks, the lower leaves will start to die as part of the regular growth cycle. If the new growth is firm and not shriveled, the succulent is likely getting enough water.

If your succulent isn't growing very quickly, it may need more water. Most succulents are fairly slow growing, but no new growth over a few weeks means you need to water more. If you've left your succulent for too long without water, the stem will also begin to constrict. It should plump out a little bit once it's watered, but it will have some permanent scarring.

Don't be afraid to experiment with your watering schedule. Each home or growing environment is unique. The selection of plants you own will also determine your watering frequency. Always err on the side of under-watering, but try different amounts of time between watering to see what works best for your plants.

signs of under-watering
- Dry, crispy leaves
- Not growing
- Stem is constricted

When a succulent gets too dry, its leaves start to shrivel.

THE RIGHT SOIL

Watering succulents properly won't do any good if you don't have the right soil. Most nurseries sell succulents in their standard potting soil, which contains mostly peat moss and doesn't drain well. Leaving succulents in this type of soil is one of the quickest ways to kill them. The right soil will allow your succulent to be watered properly and avoid root rot.

IDEAL SOIL COMPONENTS

Succulents don't like to sit in wet soil. They like water to drain out quickly, keeping the roots mostly dry. An ideal soil will include both organic and rock components. The organic component provides nutrients for the succulents, and the rock component provides stability and prevents the soil from breaking down completely. Ideally, the soil components will retain water but allow for great drainage. Coconut coir and diatomaceous earth both meet this standard.

Coconut coir comes from the husks of coconuts. It is an organic material that works as a great replacement for peat moss because it retains water but drains well. This prevents the roots of your succulent from sitting in wet soil. The coconut coir also provides some basic nutrients that succulents need to grow.

Diatomaceous earth (DE) is a type of rock that can easily absorb water. It is often used to clean up oil spills. Since it is generally pebble-like in size, it provides great drainage in a soil mixture.

The best soil for succulents is coarse and well draining.

coconut coir

diatomaceous earth

mixed soil

A blend of coconut coir and diatomaceous earth is an ideal soil mix for succulents.

PROPORTIONS

For indoor container gardens, combine two parts diatomaceous earth to one part coconut coir. This soil mixture retains enough water that the succulent roots can absorb what they need, but dries out quickly enough that they don't rot. If you tend to overwater, I'd recommend adding a little more DE than coconut coir. It dries out more quickly so your succulents won't be as likely to suffer from overwatering. On the flip side, if you tend to under-water, you can add more coconut coir than DE, so your soil stays wet a little longer. If you're just starting out, begin with two parts DE to one part coconut coir.

WHERE TO BUY SOIL COMPONENTS

Most home improvement stores such as Lowe's and Home Depot carry coconut coir during the growing season. You can also find it at various online retailers. It's often sold in a brick that needs to be soaked in water before using.

The easiest place to find diatomaceous earth is at an auto parts store. It will be marked as a product used to clean up oil spills. Kitty litter is also a form of DE, but it tends to have extra chemicals added, so it is not recommended. You can usually find DE at home improvement stores as well.

PREMIXED SOIL

If you'd rather not mix your own soil, find a soil designed for cacti and succulents or bonsai. Look for a soil mixture that has pumice, perlite, or a similar additive to help with drainage. Most premixed soils have quite a bit of peat moss, so you'll want to make sure the soil has completely dried out before watering again.

There are a lot of suggestions on soil composition for succulents from nurseries, gardeners, and succulent enthusiasts. The coconut coir and diatomaceous earth combination works well for indoor succulent growing. Feel free to experiment with other components in your soil. The most important thing to remember is that the soil needs to be well draining.

SUN EXPOSURE

One of the trickiest parts of growing succulents indoors is providing enough sunlight. Outdoors, succulents can get light all day. Indoors, windows filter out light and blinds or curtains have to be open to allow light in. Depending on the direction the windows face, you may not get enough sunlight for your succulents to thrive. Indoors, select plants that prefer less light and grow slowly. The brightest area in your home is likely the best place for your succulents.

FULL SUN OR PARTIAL SHADE?

It's important to know how much sunlight your succulent needs. Most *Echeverias* need full sun, while most *Haworthias* prefer full shade. On average, most succulents require about six hours of bright, indirect sunlight to maintain their color and shape.

If your indoor succulents need full sun, provide as much bright light as possible throughout the day. If your succulents prefer shade, you can get away with a room that gets sunlight part of the day. Generally, succulents with bright colors need more sunlight. They often turn green or lose intensity without enough light. Succulents that are naturally green in color tend to need less sunlight.

STRETCHING

An early sign that your succulents aren't getting enough sun is if the plant begins turning toward the light. It will also start to stretch out or get "leggy." You'll notice more space between the leaves, and often the new leaves will be smaller than usual. Once a succulent has stretched out, it can't go back to its original compact shape. The only way to get the arrangement back to its original shape is to cut off the top of the succulents and replant them. You can also cut down the long stems, which will start to put off new growth.

This succulent has stretched out as it reaches for light.

ARTIFICIAL LIGHTING

If you notice that your plants are starting to stretch for more light, consider using artificial lighting. Grow lights are available in all shapes, sizes, and intensities. You may need to experiment to find the right style for you.

A small space will require less light. Generally a 60-watt bulb will be enough to enhance the natural light your plant is already getting. Both fluorescent and LED lights will generally provide the right color of light to help your plants grow. You'll want to place the lights about 1 to 2 feet (0.3–0.6m) away from the plants.

Set your artificial lights on a timer or make sure they are on for 10 to 14 hours per day, during normal daylight hours. Succulents need a dark period, or night time, in order to grow properly.

A grow light can make up for natural light deficiencies.

MOVING PLANTS OUTDOORS

If your succulents need full sun, it is beneficial to move them outdoors when the weather allows. Place them in an area that gets bright indirect sunlight rather than full direct sunlight, to prevent sunburn. Direct morning sun is generally okay, as it is cooler than afternoon sun. If there is a significant difference in temperature between indoors and outdoors, you'll want to have the succulents outside for only an hour or two at a time. You can increase the time each day so that they start to acclimate to the new temperature.

Moving plants outdoors provides more airflow and better access to sunlight.

CLEANING AND TRIMMING

Keeping your succulents well maintained will help them look better and live longer. You don't have to clean and trim your succulents very often—every few months is generally enough. During their peak growing seasons you'll find your succulents need to be cared for more frequently, and less often when they're dormant.

REMOVE DIRT AND DUST

Over time you may find that your succulents accumulate dust or dirt on the leaves. To remove this, use canned air or a bulb syringe. You can also use a soft paint brush to gently brush off the dust or dirt. The paint brush may remove some of the powder coating on the succulent leaves, which is fine. It will return as the succulent continues to grow.

REMOVE DEAD LEAVES

The natural growth cycle for a succulent will leave the plant's dead leaves around the base. While it isn't a problem to leave them on, your plant will grow better and healthier without them. Removing these leaves will give the plant better airflow and may even promote new growth. It's always a good idea to remove dead leaves from newly purchased plants before placing them in a new pot or arrangement.

New plants generally form on leaf nodes, the area where the leaf was once attached. Every few weeks or months, gently remove the dead leaves from your plant. Some may still have a healthy attachment to the plant. If they do, you can leave them until they're completely shriveled, or you can remove them if the rest of the leaf is too unsightly.

If you don't remove the dead leaves from time to time, your plant will be more susceptible to bugs and rotting. Decaying plant matter is attractive to most bugs. Keeping the base of the plant cleaned up also creates better airflow, which allows the soil to dry faster and prevents rot from wet soil.

Remove dead lower leaves by pinching off gently.

Removing the dead leaves also makes it easier to see if your plant is healthy. You'll be more likely to notice shriveling in the new growth or blackening on the stem if they've been over- or under-watered. You may also see new rosettes starting to form. With the dead leaves removed, they will be able to get the sunlight they need and will grow more easily.

New rosettes form on leaf nodes.

CUT OFF NEW GROWTH

As your succulents grow, they'll likely put off new off-shoots or rosettes. If you like how full this makes your arrangement, don't worry about removing them. If the arrangement is getting too tight and is difficult to water, you can cut off some of the new growth. Since succulents propagate so easily, you can replant this new growth in an arrangement or share with friends. For more details on the best way to remove new growth, see "Propagating Succulents."

As previously mentioned, succulents grown indoors will often stretch toward the light. If you like the way your succulent looks as it gets stretched out, you can leave it. If you'd like to have a more compact arrangement again, you can cut off the top of the rosette plus any stem that is too long. Leave about 1 to 2 inches (2.5–5cm) on the base of the plant. It will put off new growth, and the rosette you cut off will eventually grow roots and can be replanted.

Cut off new growth just below a leaf.

When a succulent becomes stretched out, you can cut off the top and replant it.

FERTILIZING

Succulents don't require fertilizing to grow indoors, but they will produce more offsets and bloom more often if they do receive extra nutrients. Use a water-soluble fertilizer that is low in nitrogen and balanced in phosphorus and potassium, such as 2-7-7 plant food. Water-soluble fertilizers tend to distribute nutrients more evenly than the sticks, spikes, or slow-release options, which can easily burn succulents.

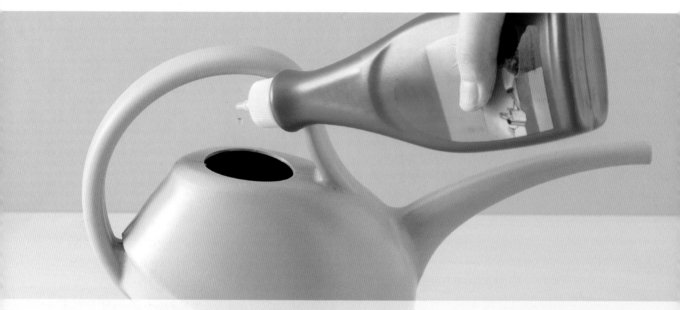

This fertilizer recommends 10 to 20 drops in 1 quart (1l) of water. Start by using the lower recommended amount.

It is best to dilute the fertilizer, even if it isn't highly concentrated. Too much concentrated fertilizer can "burn" succulents, causing patches to turn brown and possibly die. Fertilizing too frequently can cause them to grow too quickly and get stretched out. A good rule of thumb is to use half the amount of fertilizer recommended on the bottle.

Use this diluted fertilizer once in the spring and once in the fall. This should provide enough nutrients for the year. You can fertilize your succulents more often, but keep in mind that the more you fertilize, the faster your succulents will grow. If they aren't getting enough light, this can cause them to become stretched out and "leggy" quickly.

If you're growing succulents outdoors, they are likely getting more light and better airflow and can be fertilized more frequently. In their active growing season you can add the same diluted fertilizer monthly. This will encourage the plants to grow and will produce more vibrant colors. If you have just planted your succulents, give them at least a month before fertilizing to prevent any damage.

blooming

When your succulent is properly nourished and in the right environment, it may begin to bloom. Some succulents will flower annually, while others only bloom once in their lifetime. As your succulent is getting ready to bloom, you'll see a new stalk growing out of the middle of the plant. The flowers will grow on the end of the stalk and will stay alive for a few days to a few weeks, depending on the plant. Once the flowers have died, you can cut off the stalk. If you're feeling ambitious, you can harvest the seeds from the stalk and propagate them (see "Chicks" and "Seeds," under "Propagating Succulents."). A few succulents, such as the Christmas or Thanksgiving Cactus, will bloom on the end of their regular growth. You can remove the flowers once they have died. There will not be a stalk that needs to be cut or removed.

POTTING AND REPOTTING

Succulents are very tolerant of being moved to different pots. It's always exciting to find a new pot and rearrange your succulents. Sometimes when you pull out your plants, you may find new growth you hadn't noticed before.

REASONS TO REPOT

If you have the time and desire, your succulents will benefit from being repotted every year. There are also a few situations in which repotting is necessary to maintain the health of the plant.

New Succulent Purchases

Most succulents purchased at nurseries are not in soil suitable for long-term growth, so you'll definitely want to move your succulents to a new container before too long. Leaving them in the rich, wet soil will cause them to die more quickly.

Root Bound

As your succulents grow, they'll put off more and more roots and begin to fill up the pot. Often newly purchased succulents will be root bound, meaning the roots are tightly packed together and fill most of the pot they are in. Any time you see roots coming out the bottom of the pot, the succulent is ready for a new home. The roots need more space to grow so they get better airflow and have more access to the water they need.

Repot newly purchased succulents as soon as possible.

Bug Infestation

At the first sign of bugs, you'll want to repot immediately. Often bugs will hide in the soil and are hard to see. The soil could also be attracting the bugs, so it's best to get rid of it and sanitize the pot before starting again.

Outgrown Container

If you notice your plants getting too big for the pot they are in, it's time to repot. Succulents grow more slowly in very tight arrangements, and will almost stop growing once their roots have filled the pot. For the health of your succulents, it's best to remove them and plant them in something a little larger. If you don't want them to get any bigger, they can keep growing in the smaller container, but they may not continue to be as healthy.

THE BEST TIME OF YEAR TO REPOT

The best time of year to do repotting is just before the active growing season for your succulents (see "When to Water Succulents" to determine the active growing season). This will give them plenty of time to recover from the shock of being replanted. They will also be able to intake more water and are less likely to rot. If you do replant your succulents at the end of their growing season, be very careful not to overwater.

When a succulent gets too large for its container, it needs to be repotted.

HOW TO REPOT

Potting succulents is fairly straightforward, but these tips will ensure that your plants continue to thrive after repotting.

Remove soil from the roots before repotting the succulents.

Place the largest succulent in the center of the pot before adding smaller succulents around it.

1 **Remove soil.** As you pull your succulents out of their original pots, remove as much soil as you can. This is especially important for newly purchased succulents. As you remove the soil, check for any problems with the roots and examine the plant for bugs.

2 **Remove roots.** As you remove the soil, it is totally fine to remove some of the roots of your succulent. If the succulent is root bound, it may actually benefit from the removal. Removing the roots shocks the plant and encourages new growth. You don't want to rip off all of the roots, but don't worry if you remove quite a bit. Your succulent will survive.

3 **Remove dead leaves and separate new growth.** If you haven't trimmed your plants in a while, you'll want to remove any dead leaves from the succulent. You can also pull off or separate any new growth that you'd like to plant elsewhere.

4 **Watch the leaves.** As you are potting, though, keep an eye on the leaves and avoid breaking them or knocking them off. It will take a while for new leaves to grow and fill in. Some succulents, such as *Sedum morganianum* and *Sedum rubrotinctum*, have very delicate leaves that can fall off from just a slight bump. Remember that this is normal and be as careful as you can.

5 **Work inside out.** It's generally easiest to plant the succulents in the middle of the container first. Place the largest succulents first and fill in with the smaller succulents. If you have plants that will hang over the edge of the pot, put those in near the end and use other "filler" succulents over the roots to hold them in place.

WAIT TO WATER

It's best to wait a day or two before watering your newly planted succulents. This will give the roots some time to heal before being flooded with water. It's also best to keep the succulents in a mild or protected climate for a couple of days. Really hot weather or sudden cold can be more than the succulent can handle in its freshly potted state.

working with cacti and sharp succulents

Use newspaper to hold a cactus while moving it into place.

Many succulents are smooth and easy to handle, but some have sharp spines that can be tricky to work with. There are several techniques you can use when handling cacti and other spiny succulents.

Wear gloves. Thick gloves with rubber coating are the best. Leather gloves will protect against some spines, but they can still be easily penetrated.

Use tongs. Rubber-tipped tongs can be used on the body of the plant. Squeeze gently because they can still puncture the leaves. You can also use tongs on the root ball, but be careful that the plant doesn't tip over and fall on your hands or arms as you move it.

Use a newspaper or towel. This technique works very well, especially for cacti such as *Opuntia microdasys albata,* which have hundreds of tiny spines that easily get stuck in skin. Wrap the cactus in newspaper, a towel, or even cardboard. Make sure your material is long enough to wrap around the plant and leave some extra to hold onto. If it's thick enough, you can hold onto the wrapped portion of the plant. If the spines still come through the paper, use the excess as a handle to guide the plant into place.

COMMON PESTS AND PROBLEMS

Succulents aren't prone to bugs or diseases, but if you don't care for the plants properly, they'll make their way in. In most cases the plant can be treated and saved, but sometimes the infected plant puts nearby plants at risk. Here are some of the common pests and problems with growing succulents indoors.

Spray the bugs with a dish soap solution to kill them.

GNATS

While gnats won't do anything to bother your succulents, they reproduce quickly and can be annoying to have in your home. Gnats love wet soil. If you start to have a gnat problem, you are most likely overwatering your succulents and their pots don't have enough drainage.

Gnats lay eggs in the soil, so let the soil dry out for several days. If the gnats return, spray the soil with several drops of lemon-scented dish soap in about a quart (1l) water.

This should kill any eggs but will not harm the succulent. You can also pour a small amount of 70 percent rubbing alcohol on the soil.

Another technique for getting rid of gnats is to place a small dish of apple cider vinegar with a few drops of dish soap near your succulents. The gnats will be attracted to the sweet smell of the vinegar, and the dish soap will kill them on contact.

These mealybugs have stunted the new growth of this plant as they've eaten the leaves.

MEALYBUGS

These nasty bugs are the most common pest problem for succulents grown indoors. The first sign of mealybugs is a white, fluffy substance on leaves or in crevices between the leaves of your plant. Mealybugs themselves are tiny and brown and very hard to spot. As soon as you see mealybugs on one of your plants, move it away from any others. Mealybugs spread quickly and it's easy for all of your plants to become infested.

To get rid of mealybugs, spray or pour 70 percent rubbing alcohol anywhere you see the bugs on your succulent. Alcohol can burn or damage the leaves, so rinse them with water about 10 to 15 minutes after application. This will allow the alcohol to kill what's there without damaging your succulent. You may want to spray it with alcohol every few days to ensure you've killed all the bugs.

If the mealybugs don't go away, repot and replace the soil. Often, they will nest down in the soil around the stem and roots. Getting rid of the infested soil is the best way to eliminate this problem. When you remove the plant, spray the roots with alcohol. If you'd like to avoid repotting, pour alcohol over the soil for the next few waterings to kill any eggs that have been laid in the soil.

Damage from mealybugs usually looks like stunted and misshapen growth. They target the new growth of the plant and like to hide in the areas between the leaves and stem. If your succulent is severely infested with mealybugs, you may want to consider throwing away the plant rather than putting other plants at risk.

SUNBURN

Succulents can be damaged from too much sunlight or direct light that is too hot. Your succulents can get sunburn from being too close to a window that gets direct sunlight. They can also burn easily from being in full sun outdoors for too long if they aren't acclimated to the heat.

Initial sunburns are white, and it looks like the plant is turning pale. At this point, bringing it into the shade can prevent further damage and scarring. Most likely, though, you'll see dark spots or even brown, crispy leaves if it gets burned severely. The scars from sunburns won't go away or heal. Eventually, as the plant grows, those leaves will die and fall off.

ROT

There are several reasons a succulent will begin to rot, but the most common reason is overwatering. Some diseases, such as *Aloe* rust or black mold, can cause succulents to rot as well, but these are quite rare, especially when growing indoors. The earliest sign of rot is softening of the leaves. As it progresses you'll start to see black spots on the stem or leaves. Eventually the black from the rot will spread to other areas of the plant.

It is hard to save a succulent from rot, especially if it gets very far. The best way is to use a sterile knife or scissors to cut off the top of the plant above any black spots. Check the inside of the stem to ensure this cutting doesn't have any blackening inside. If it does, continue to cut off the stem until there are no signs of blackening. Wait a few days for the end to callous and then replant the cutting.

Too much much sun can cause browning or sunburn on succulent leaves.

Blackening and rot along the stem of a succulent is caused by overwatering.

ANIMALS

You'll find that animals are quite attracted to succulents. Mice, raccoons, rabbits, birds, and deer have all been known to take a bite of outdoor succulents from time to time. They can be hard to deter, but the best way to do so is to keep the succulents in a protected area where they are hard to get to.

Slugs and snails can also be a problem outdoors. The smooth skin of succulents is easy for snails to eat. They can eat succulents quickly. You'll notice some slime as well as an open wound on your succulent. Slug bait is the easiest way to eliminate this problem. Just spread a little on the soil surrounding your succulents.

You'll likely have problems with your cats and dogs indoors. While some succulents are poisonous and animals stay away, most are quite tasty. It is difficult to keep these animals away from succulents. Keep your succulents up high and out of reach of your pets.

Ants can be a problem both indoors and outdoors. If you see them indoors, they likely caught a ride on some new succulents you purchased. Ants won't eat your succulents, but they do like to eat the white webs mealybugs create. They end up spreading the mealybugs around and make the mealybug problem worse. You can use traps or other common methods for removing ants to help with this problem.

Pets love succulents, so keep them out of reach.

PROPAGATING SUCCULENTS

One of the most interesting things about succulents is how easily they propagate. Propagation can be a great way to expand your collection. There are several different ways to propagate succulents, and each is a little different. The main types of propagation use leaves, cuttings, chicks (also called offsets, babies, or pups), and seeds.

LEAVES

Propagating from leaves is one of the most amazing types of succulent propagation. You can simply remove a leaf from a succulent, place it on soil, water frequently, and within a few weeks, roots will start to emerge and a tiny new succulent will form on the end of the leaf! Some succulents, such as Mother of Thousands, actually grow babies on the edges of their leaves. When they are big enough, they fall off and grow on their own.

Many succulents can propagate from individual leaves.

CUTTINGS

Most succulents can be grown from cuttings. The technique for taking the cutting varies slightly depending on the plant. Once the cutting is taken, it needs to dry out for a couple of days. Then, with frequent watering it will form roots at the base of the stem and continue to grow. This type of propagation is nice because you will end up with two (or more, depending on the number of cuttings) established plants in just a matter of weeks.

Taking cuttings is a quick way to multiply your succulent collection.

Many succulents reproduce on their own by putting off new "chicks."

CHICKS

You may be familiar with the term "hens and chicks." This refers to varieties of succulents that put off tiny new plants all on their own, such as *Sempervivums* and *Echeverias*. Both of these succulent types tend to put off several new chicks every year. These chicks form roots much more easily than cuttings and grow very quickly. They can be removed from the mother hen or left to grow where they are. Eventually, the mother hen will die, but she will leave plenty of chicks before she does!

SEEDS

Propagating succulents from seeds is the most difficult way to generate new succulents and is the least reliable. Most succulents will flower at least once during their lifetime. Some succulents, such as *Agaves*, will put off just one flower in their lifetime and die after it blooms. The seeds are harvested from these flowers. They have to dry out before they can be planted. Succulents grown from seeds do not always perfectly resemble their parent plant. The pollination causes changes to occur and the result can be quite exciting!

However you decide to propagate your succulents, you're sure to be in for a treat. It can be quite addicting, and before you know it you'll have a house full of plants! There's something so rewarding about getting more plants without spending any more money. Every succulent will propagate at least one of these ways and maybe more.

PROPAGATING FROM LEAVES

There isn't a hard-and-fast rule to determine whether a succulent will propagate from leaves. In general, succulents with thick leaves that attach to a stem (rather than an Aloe, which doesn't have a stem) will propagate from leaves. However, there are a few thinner-leaved succulents that can propagate from leaves too, such as Kalanchoe marnieriana. A few succulents that propagate easily from leaves include Aeonium 'Kiwi,' Graptoveria 'Fred Ives,' Kalanchoe tomentosa, Sedum morganianum, and Sedum rubrotinctum. The last two are incredibly prolific from leaf propagation.

REMOVING THE LEAF

The best way to remove a leaf to use for propagation is to gently twist it off. Pulling or pushing down can sometimes cause the leaf to break. Broken leaves don't generally propagate well. Lay these newly removed leaves out to dry for a couple of days. The end needs to heal, or callous, before you water them. Watering too soon can cause the leaf to rot. Lay the leaves on soil and don't bury the ends. Once the ends have calloused over you can begin watering.

Gently twist a leaf to remove it for propagation.

WATERING

Keep the soil under your leaves damp but not soaking wet. This is one time when it's okay to mist your succulents. You can mist the soil every day to make sure it stays moist, although it's not a problem for the soil to dry out for a little bit.

Keep the soil moist until roots and new plants start to form. Once the roots can reach into the soil and the new plant is about ½ inch (1.25cm) in size, gradually cut back on watering. As the plants continue to grow, you'll slowly begin to water them as you would full-grown succulents: give them a good soak, and then water again when they dry out.

Lay out leaves on soil and keep the soil moist for propagating.

SUCCESS RATE

Keep in mind that not all of the leaves will actually propagate. About 50 percent or less of the leaves will produce new plants. For your first attempt at leaf propagation it's best to have a lot of leaves from a variety of plants. This will give you an idea of which plants propagate best in your environment.

Some leaves will put off a lot of new roots but never a plant. This can be frustrating but is very normal. You can rip off some of the roots to try and shock the leaf into growing a plant. This works occasionally, but most often the leaf just keeps putting off roots.

As the new succulent gets stronger, the original leaf will begin to shrivel and die.

REPLANTING

After several weeks or months of growing, the original leaf will begin to shrivel and die. Keep the new plant in the same place for another couple of weeks. When the new succulent is about 1 inch (2.5cm) in size and has a strong root system, you can move it to a new pot. Transplanting these babies earlier can cause them to die quickly because they aren't strong enough to tolerate the same watering schedule as a larger plant.

TEMPERATURE AND TIMELINE

An indoor environment is great for propagating succulents from leaves as well as cuttings, pups, and seeds. Avoid placing the leaves in hot, direct sunlight. Warm, bright shade or just inside a window indoors is the best location. It can take several weeks for succulent leaves to show signs of new growth. Warmer temperatures encourage the succulents to grow faster, and sometimes leaves can put off roots within a few days. Again, it's a great idea to experiment to determine the best environment for propagating succulents from leaves in your home.

PROPAGATING FROM CUTTINGS

One of the easiest ways to propagate succulents is from cuttings. Nearly all succulents can be propagated from cuttings, so it's a great way to expand your collection. Many plants will put off new growth over time. You can take cuttings of this new growth and plant it somewhere new. You can also take cuttings of plants that have stretched out from lack of sunlight.

Use sterile clippers or scissors to take succulent cuttings.

Remove a few leaves from your cutting to provide a place for roots to grow.

CLEAN CUT

A cutting will grow best if it's a clean cut. Use a sterile knife or scissors to cut off the top of your succulent or a new offshoot. If you are removing the top of the plant, make the cut just below a leaf. If you are cutting off new growth, cut as close to the main stem of the succulent as possible.

REMOVE THE LEAVES

If the succulent you are working with has a stem and leaves, remove a few of the lower leaves. The new roots will grow from the bottom of the stem as well as from the leaf nodes where the leaves were once attached. You can then save those leaves and try propagating them.

ALLOW TO DRY

Leave the cuttings in a warm, shady place to dry for 3 to 4 days. The end of the cutting needs to heal and callous over before being placed in soil. If you notice significant shriveling after 1 to 2 days, go ahead and water.

WATERING

Once the end of the cutting has calloused over, you can plant it in soil. Bury the bottom of the cutting in the soil enough that the cutting will stand on its own. Begin watering every few days. Keep the soil damp but not soaking wet. After a few days or possibly weeks, roots will begin to form and you can then start to water the cutting as if it were an established plant.

KEEP THE ORIGINAL PLANT

If you took your cutting from the top of your plant (perhaps it was growing too tall and leggy), keep caring for the original plant. Remove one or two of the leaves from the top of the stem. Keep the lower leaves so they can absorb sunlight for the plant. Within a few weeks, new plant heads will begin to form on the stem. You don't need to change your watering schedule or care of this plant. If you cut off new growth, it's not likely that new growth will form where you took the cutting from the original plant. If you left some leaves from the new growth (rather than cutting next to the main stem), it is possible you'll see some new sprouts.

Let the cutting sit out for 3 to 4 days before planting in soil.

New growth will form on the plant from which the cutting was removed.

PROPAGATING FROM CHICKS

There really isn't much to propagating from chicks (also called pups, offsets, or babies). The succulent has already done the work! Sempervivums propagate from chicks. The mother "hen" will put off several new chicks on stolons, or long horizontal stems. These chicks grow roots of their own. Aloes and Haworthias also "pup" or offset easily. Instead of sending off chicks on a stolon, the Aloe pups clump around the mother plant.

Cut the stolon to remove chicks from the mother plant.

Gently pull the pups away from the mother plant.

REMOVING CHICKS

Once a chick has roots of its own, the stolon can be cut and the chick planted elsewhere. The chicks may need a little more water and protection from sun until they get used to surviving on their own.

REMOVING PUPS

Pups can be removed from the mother plant by gently tugging or pulling them apart. As you pull them off, make sure some roots are attached to the pup. While it can survive without the roots, it will grow more quickly and easily with roots already attached. You can water these as you would an established plant because their root system is already established.

MOTHER PLANTS

The mother plants of these pupping succulents will die eventually, but not as a result of the chick being removed. Generally, the mother plant is unaffected by removing offsets. It will continue to produce more until the end of its life cycle.

PROPAGATING FROM SEEDS

Growing succulents from seeds is the most difficult type of propagation. Most of the time, less than half of the seeds will sprout and even fewer will survive to be full plants. There is also an element of surprise when propagating from seeds. Frequently the new plants that form will have slightly different characteristics than the parent plant.

COLLECTING THE SEEDS

The seeds for succulents are collected from the flower stalk of the plant. If you plan to harvest the seeds, allow the flower stalk to start to shrivel and then cut off the stalk. Place the stalk in a brown paper bag in a dry place to allow the seeds and stalk to dry out. Shake the bag from time to time to help the seeds fall out of their pods. Allow the seeds to dry for a few months before planting.

Cut off the flower stalk and place it in a brown paper bag to dry.

PLANTING THE SEEDS

Succulent seeds are sown and germinated similarly to other plants. The easiest way to germinate seeds is in a plastic tray with a clear plastic lid. Fill the tray with succulent soil and mist it until it is damp. Sprinkle the seeds on top of the soil. Put the cover on the tray and place it in a warm area with indirect sunlight.

Once the seeds have sprouted and the plants are easily visible, you can remove the cover. Mist the soil when needed to keep the soil moist. The little sprouts will need to stay moist until they have put out strong roots that can withstand drought. Cut back on watering as the sprouts get larger. Eventually you can water as you would an established plant. It can take months and sometimes over a year for the seedlings to grow to an inch (2.5cm) in size.

Lay seeds on top of soil in a plastic tray with a lid to germinate.

3

SELECTING & ARRANGING SUCCULENTS

One of the best things about succulents is that you can pair almost any two varieties and they will look great together. With so many different colors and textures, it's fun to experiment with new combinations. Selecting a beautiful container can be just as much fun as selecting the succulents. Traditional pots come in all shapes, sizes, and colors, but you can also try more unusual containers. Succulents look good in just about anything, even an old shoe! You've probably seen some pretty cool arrangements with succulents, and now you'll be able to create your own. It can be daunting at first, but soon you'll feel like an expert.

PURCHASING SUCCULENTS

Buying succulents is one of the most exciting parts of creating a succulent garden. There are so many gorgeous options to choose from. However, it can be overwhelming, especially if you're a novice gardener. Where should you go to buy them? What varieties should you choose? The following tips should help make your buying experience simple and fun.

LOCAL OPTIONS

Regardless of where you live, you'll likely be able to find succulents locally. The selection may be limited, but you should be able to find something. Stores such as Lowe's, Home Depot, and Walmart have a surprisingly good selection of succulents, especially during the summer months. Succulents tend to be grouped with tropical and indoor plants, so start by looking in that area. Most of the prices at these big-box stores will be pretty reasonable.

During the summer, you'll likely be able to find succulents at your local nursery. They generally carry only a few varieties, but they may be larger than the box stores and at a better price. You can also look for a specialty store to find more unusual succulents. This will likely be the most expensive option, but if you're looking for a specific plant and want to buy locally, this may be the best option.

There are several advantages to shopping locally as opposed to ordering online. I prefer shopping locally whenever possible because I can pick the exact specimen I want. Also, you don't have to pay for shipping, so the plants are generally less expensive than they are online. It's also nice to be able to talk with a salesperson and ask questions about the plants you're buying.

A disadvantage to buying locally is the lack of selection. Unless you live in an area that is ideal for growing succulents (such as Southern California), the selection available may be limited to the more popular succulents. If you're looking for something specific, you may have a hard time finding what you want.

ONLINE OPTIONS

Selection is the major advantage to buying online. Between specialty online shops, Etsy, Facebook groups, and major online nurseries, you're almost guaranteed to find what you want. The downside is they tend to be expensive, especially when you factor in shipping.

Shipping and delivery of succulents also introduces some risk. Packaging varies from store to store, and it's hard to know what you'll get. I've received fragile succulents in perfect condition, but I've also received pretty tough succulents in less than ideal condition. Reading reviews about the seller will help you determine how well the plants are packaged.

It can also be hard to know exactly what you're getting when you're buying online. Most places show a generic picture of the plant but not the exact specimen you'll be receiving. Some sellers, such as those on Etsy or in Facebook groups, may be able to send you a picture of the exact plant you'll be getting. If you're just looking to start your own collection, it's not as important that the succulent be in perfect condition. If you're doing a boutonnière or giving succulents as a gift, not knowing the exact state of the plant can be a risk.

Buying succulents online is very convenient. While there are some challenges, most of these can be overcome once you've found the right seller. Check the "Resources" section for some of my favorite places to buy succulents online.

SELECTING SUCCULENTS

When you're shopping for succulents, you might wonder what makes one specimen better than another. As long as the plant is healthy, any specimen can be a good choice. But to get the most for your money, here are some things to look out for.

CHECK FOR SIGNS OF ROT OR BUGS

Most of the succulents you'll find should be healthy. However, it pays to look for warning signs. Avoid anything that seems to be wilting. Generally this means the plant has been overwatered and is starting to die. It's possible it has been under-watered, but most succulents are going to be in a rich soil that doesn't drain well, so they are more likely to be suffering from overwatering.

Keep an eye out for early signs of mealybugs as well. You might see some actual cobwebs from spiders and that is fine, but mealybugs have a sticky white web that sticks right to the leaves. You'll usually see it in the middle of the plant where leaves connect to each other or the stem. Sometimes sediment from water can resemble mealybugs, so it's a good idea to check with a salesperson. It's possible to save plants that are suffering from rot or mealybugs, but I don't recommend trying unless you've been growing succulents for a while.

CHECK FOR SCARS ON LEAVES

Once a succulent has been scarred or damaged it doesn't heal and disappear. Eventually the leaf will die (or you can pull it off) and then you won't see it anymore. It's not a problem for the leaf to have scars, but if you don't like the way it looks, try to find one with less scarring. Some *Haworthias* tend to have brown tips from time to time. This is normal and is not cause for concern. You can still try to find one with fewer brown tips, though.

SEEK OUT MULTIPLE PLANTS OR ROSETTES

My favorite thing to do when shopping for succulents is to look for a pot with multiple plants. You can separate them when you get home, giving you more succulents for your money. For something rosette shaped, look for a plant with as many rosettes as possible. My best find was a $5 *Echeveria* 'Afterglow' with one giant rosette and seven medium rosettes attached. Looking for rosettes or bonus plants makes plant buying like a treasure hunt.

CONSIDER YOUR CONTAINER

There is a lot that goes into selecting a container for your succulents. I highly recommend taking your container with you when you select your plants to ensure that they look amazing together. That said, succulents tend to look great in just about anything!

CHOOSING THE RIGHT CONTAINER

Selecting a pot for your succulent is almost as much fun as picking out the succulents! There are a variety of shapes, sizes, and materials for pots, and most will work well for succulents. Succulents generally have shallow roots so they thrive in short, wide pots as well as tall, skinny pots.

DRAINAGE HOLES

The pot you select for your succulents must have a drainage hole. As mentioned previously, succulents need the water to flow out of the pot to prevent rot. If possible, it's best to find a pot that already has a hole, but if you want to use a container that doesn't have a hole, see "How to Adapt a Non-Draining Container."

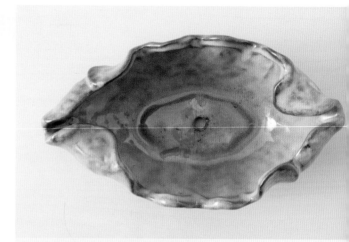

MATERIALS

There are four basic materials from which pots are made: ceramic, plastic, metal, and glass. While succulents can grow in any of these types of pots, ceramic is generally the best option.

Ceramic

Ceramic pots are porous, which allows air to flow through the pot, causing the soil to dry out faster. Unglazed terra cotta pots are probably the best material for succulents as they are extremely breathable and allow water to evaporate quickly. The downside of a ceramic pot is fragility. If it's dropped once, it will most likely break.

Plastic and Metal

Plastic and metal are both durable and less breakable alternatives to ceramic pots. They aren't as breathable, so well-draining soil and a drainage hole are especially important. Plastic pots come in a lot of fun colors and varieties and work well for growing succulents. Keep in mind that metal will change temperatures with the environment. If the pot gets too hot from direct sunlight, this can cause the roots of your succulents (or leaves, if they are touching the pot) to burn. Metal is best in a temperate climate. It also has the disadvantage of rusting over time, which is also not good for succulents.

Glass

Glass is the trickiest material for a succulent container. It's extremely rare for a glass container to have a drainage hole and glass is not breathable. If you are planting in a glass container, realize that your succulents will not last very long. Even with careful watering they are likely to die from rot due to water buildup in the bottom of the container. If you like the idea of planting succulents in glass, consider adding a drainage hole to extend the life of your succulents.

More unusual pots complement the funky shapes of some succulents.

This pot with vertical lines mimics the vertical leaves of the *Kalanchoe tomentosa.*

SHAPE AND TEXTURE

Succulents will grow well in just about any shape of pot. When you're choosing your pot, consider what plants you'll be using and try to select a pot that either mimics the shape of the plants or provides contrast.

You can also look at the texture of the pot and compare that to the plants you'll be using. If your succulents are mostly circular in shape, look for a round pot that has a circular form to create repetition in your design. There can even be subtle texture that reflects the plant you're using.

shopping for pots

The pot you choose for your succulent arrangement plays a big part in the overall look and feel of the design. Whenever possible, select your plants and your pot at the same time. If you have a succulent that you absolutely love, bring it with you when you're looking for a pot. You'll be sure to come away with an amazing pot that enhances the beauty of the plant.

Try to match the size of the
succulents to the size of the pot.

This energetic arrangement repeats
the vibrant colors from the pot.

SIZE

Depending on where you purchase your plants, you're
likely to come away with relatively small specimens.
While many succulents can grow quite large, you'll want
to plant them in something that gives them some room to
grow but isn't too big. For growing indoors, a smaller pot
will be more versatile and can be moved more easily. You'll
also want to consider the height of your succulents relative
to the height of the pot you choose. If you have short succulents, you probably won't choose a really tall pot. Look
for something that complements the size of your plants.

COLOR

There are so many gorgeous pots available with a wide
range of colors, both bright and subdued. You can select
succulents that are the same color as your pot or that
contrast with it. There are a variety of color schemes
that you can follow, which are covered in the section on
"Arranging by Color." While succulents will look great
in just about any color of container, your arrangement is
much more likely to impress if the container coordinates
with your plants.

USING TOP DRESSINGS

You may have seen succulent arrangements that have pebbles, crushed stones, or other material covering the top of the soil. This material is called a top dressing and it's an often overlooked but important part of creating an arrangement. Adding the right top dressing can make the arrangement really shine and seem more cohesive. There are numerous options for top dressings, from flashy to subtle. Use whatever works best to enhance the plants you've selected for your arrangement.

A top dressing creates a finished look and adds color and texture to the arrangement.

This purple top dressing complements, but does not distract from, the colors of the succulent and the pot.

FUNCTION

Top dressings don't just look pretty; they also serve a purpose. Using something like rocks or glass gems on top of the soil prevents soil dust from coming up each time you water and keeps the arrangement looking clean and fresh. A top dressing also enhances the arrangement by providing color, texture, and shape. In the same way the color of the pot affects the look of the arrangement, a top dressing adds a subtle touch of color to really make the succulent stand out.

THE RIGHT FIT

There are a variety of options for top dressings. They range from moss to glass to pebbles and other stones. You can find different sizes and colors of pea gravel at a local rock supplier. You might find warm colors, cool grays, and even black pebbles. Aquarium gravel comes in every color of the rainbow. Crushed seashells work well for an under-the-sea look.

When you're selecting your top dressing, keep in mind that you want it to complement the succulents and not draw attention to itself. Often using a neutral color or a color from the arrangement is the best way to go.

TOOLS

Getting the top dressing in the right places can be a bit tricky. A few tools will help you get the look you want: a soft-bristled brush, a long scoop, and long-handled tweezers. These items can all be found at your local craft store.

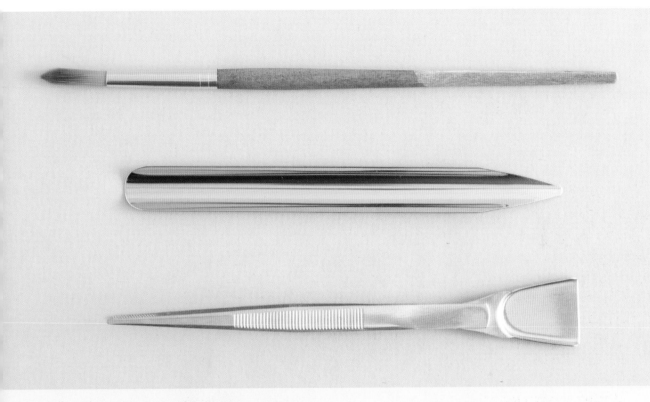

The tweezers and scoop shown here were purchased as a set and are normally used for scooping up small beads.

A scoop can be used to add the top dressing.

The scoop works well to get rocks and gems into hard-to-reach places. The tweezers are great for placing moss or removing rocks from between leaves. The brush is useful for removing top dressings from between the leaves of your succulents. You can also use it to smooth out finer top dressings, such as sand.

HOW TO ADAPT A NON-DRAINING CONTAINER

You've found the perfect pot for your succulents, but then you realize it doesn't have a drainage hole. Don't worry! You can add a drainage hole to almost any container. While it's more difficult than using a pot that already has a hole, adding a drainage hole allows you to use a variety of new pots and other containers for succulents.

TOOLS

Adding a drainage hole is all about having the right tools. The right tool will be different depending on the material of your container. You'll find that some materials are easier to add drainage to than others.

For **metal containers,** you can simply use a hammer and nail. Use a nail that is about ¹⁄₁₆-inch (1.5mm) wide. Pound holes all along the bottom of the container. This will provide much better drainage than a single, large hole. You can also use a drill for metal containers.

It's easiest to add drainage to **plastic containers** by using a drill. You can generally use a standard ¹⁄₁₆-inch (1.5mm)

drill bit. Drill multiple holes along the bottom of the pot, the same as you'd do with a metal container.

Ceramic and **glass** are a bit trickier. To add a drainage hole to a glass vase or ceramic pot you'll need a diamond-tip drill bit. These are about $15 at your local hardware store, but may be less expensive online. Using a diamond-tip drill bit is a little different than using a regular bit. You'll need to have water on hand and should wear safety goggles when drilling. Some pots are much easier to drill through than others, so be patient and don't try to rush the drilling process.

DRILLING WITH A DIAMOND-TIP DRILL BIT

1 Turn the pot upside down. Spray or pour water on the bottom of the pot until it pools. Keep the surface of the pot wet the entire time you are drilling.

2 Begin drilling slowly and at an angle. The drill will move around, but keep it as steady as possible. Use enough force to keep the drill in place, but don't push too hard.

3 Once you've created a groove, begin moving the drill to a vertical position, perpendicular to the pot. Increase the drilling speed and keep an even pressure.

4 As you get close to completely drilling through the pot, lighten the force on the drill. You can easily break a pot by hitting the bottom of it with the drill when it finally goes all the way through.

USING UNUSUAL CONTAINERS

One of the awesome things about succulents is that, due to their shallow root system and drought tolerance, they can be planted in unusual containers. You can plant succulents in just about anything you can think of: a scrap of wood, a birdhouse, even an old pan or shoe!

DRAINAGE

As with any container selection, you need to make sure your unusual container has a drainage hole. If you plan on your arrangement being temporary, you can probably get away without a drainage hole. Otherwise, you risk losing your plants and possibly ruining your container. Metal containers can rust and rot out, and wood planters can also rot out if the water doesn't drain. You're also more likely to attract bugs and diseases. See "How to Adapt a Non-Draining Container" for tips on adding drainage to your containers if they don't already have a hole.

SOIL OR NO SOIL?

Succulents survive surprisingly well with little or no soil. If you're planting in something like driftwood, a little sphagnum moss will work as a replacement for soil. Sometimes your planting may be so tight that there isn't room for anything other than succulents.

If possible, it's best to use soil, but your succulents will be just fine without it. Without soil, you'll want to make sure the roots stay out of direct sunlight. Water the roots directly if possible or make sure the water can run down onto the roots. A soilless arrangement can last for several years if the roots are protected. It will also benefit from semi-annual fertilizing as soil generally provides some nutrients for the succulents.

LIFESPAN

It's surprising how long succulents can grow in something other than a pot. While they may not get much bigger or produce very many new plants, succulents can last for a few years in most containers. With proper care and maintenance, your succulents will stay alive and keep looking great.

HAVE FUN

Don't be afraid to try new things and really experiment with your containers. Succulents are pretty forgiving and will grow almost anywhere. Take a look around the house and see what you can repurpose as a succulent planter!

ARRANGING BY HEIGHT

There are a variety of guidelines for designing container arrangements. One of the more fundamental techniques is to use height as the main design element. There are a number of ways height can be incorporated into a design.

THRILLERS, FILLERS, AND SPILLERS

A common and simple way to arrange plants is by using the "thriller, filler, and spiller" technique. The basic idea here is to have a variety of plants with various heights.

You start your arrangement by placing a "thriller" plant. A thriller is something tall and striking, often spikey. It's what gets your attention when you're looking at the arrangement. These could be *Aloes, Agaves,* or *Haworthias,* depending on the size of your arrangement.

Next, you'll add in "filler" plants. These are generally lower plants that fill the bulk of the arrangement. They complement or contrast with the thriller plant while adding continued interest and flow to the arrangement. Some filler plants include *Echeverias* and *Sedums.*

The "spiller" plants are the lowest plants in the arrangement and "spill" over. They break up the visual edge of the pot and give the arrangement a finished look. *Senecio rowleyanus* and *Senecio radicans* are great spillers.

UNIFORM HEIGHT

Another technique used for arrangements is using a uniform height. Arranging this way gives more equal focus to each of the plants and draws attention to the variations in shape, texture, and color. You can do this using a variety of lower-growing plants such as *Sempervivums* and *Echeverias* or by using a variety of tall and more upward-growing succulents such as *Portulacaria afra* and *Sansevieria cylindrica*.

PROPORTION

You can also design your arrangement by using the height of the pot as your guide. Succulent designer Cindy Davison recommends taking the height of your pot and multiplying it by 1½, then using that measurement as the tallest point in your arrangement. This creates a very balanced arrangement that is pleasing to the eye.

You can also design arrangements using the principle of thirds. For this type of arrangement, the height of the pot would be one-third of the entire arrangement and the plants would be the other two-thirds. You could also do the opposite proportions and have the pot be two-thirds and the plants one-third. This type of arrangement also creates a sense of balance and is visually compelling.

ARRANGING BY COLOR

Succulents come in every color of the rainbow, so it's easy to make a beautiful arrangement based on basic color principles. Pottery also comes in many colors and you can select succulents based on the colors in your pot. Whatever you choose, arranging succulents by color is a fun way to design.

THE COLOR WHEEL

Consider the color wheel when selecting your container and arranging your succulents. Complementary colors are opposite each other on the color wheel, such as purple and yellow or green and red. Monochromatic colors are tints and shades of the same color, such as light and dark green. Analogous colors are next to each other on the color wheel, such as blue and green or purple and red.

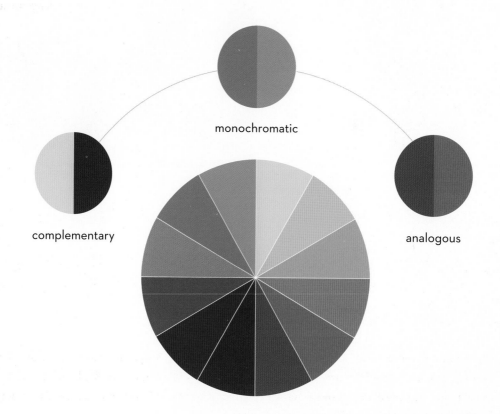

monochromatic

complementary

analogous

COMPLEMENTARY

Some of the best arrangements I've seen use succulents of complementary colors. Blues and oranges bring out the best in each other. Reds and greens are found together naturally on a wide variety of succulents. Purples and yellows can be done as well, although they are harder to find. Using complementary colors in an arrangement draws the attention to color. The contrast keeps the eye moving throughout the design. It's a great way to create a striking arrangement.

MONOCHROMATIC

Using plants of the same color with various tints and shades, as well as different shapes and textures, creates subtle visual interest. The focus is on the variations between the plants and isn't as much about the color. With such a variety of green succulents, you're sure to find a range of textures to incorporate into your design. The viewer will be able to appreciate the details of the plants and how they all differ from one another.

ANALOGOUS

Using an analogous color scheme gives you a lot of
options. You can use any colors that are next to each
other on the color wheel. The pot can also play a part
in the color scheme. You can use two, three, or four
colors depending on how much color variation you
want in the arrangement. This color scheme adds
interest and contrast with color while still maintain-
ing a sense of unity and flow.

MIMIC THE CONTAINER

A great way to design a cohesive arrangement is by using the colors, textures, and shapes from your pot or container and incorporating those elements into the design using succulents. Look for the strongest colors and for colors that just appear in accents or creases in the pottery. You can use the main color from the pot as an accent color in the plants or use it as the main color in the plants to create more repetition.

PERFECT PAIRINGS

While nearly all succulents look great paired together, there are some that look better together than others. You'll also find that certain pots will really make your plants stand out while others might distract. This section provides guidance on creating perfect pairings and examples to inspire your own succulent arrangements.

This *Graptopetalum paraguayense,* also called Ghost Plant, has subtle changes in color, creating an overall appearance of purple. The geode stone mimics the shape of the leaves and adds visual interest to the arrangement. Various shades of darker purple in the top dressing highlight the color variation in the plant while adding a great backdrop to help the plant stand out. A purple pot ties together the whole monochromatic arrangement.

Echeveria 'Cubic Frost' has very light tones with hints of purple, blue, and green. The light blue-green pot complements the color of the succulent perfectly. Lines in the pot mimic the upside-down V-shape of the leaves. The final touch of light-colored sea glass as a top dressing keeps the whole arrangement's appearance soft and cohesive.

This combination of succulent and pottery emphasizes the form of the *Sanseveria trifasciata hahnii*. The color and texture of the succulent leaves is also repeated with the light brown and green in the artichoke pot. The top dressing repeats the colors found in the pot.

Notocactus rudibueneckerii is the star of this arrangement. The white in the pot picks up the white of the cactus, and the clumps of clay mimic the spots of white on the plant. The tones in both the cactus and the pot are cool, keeping the arrangement cohesive.

The green of this pot very strongly repeats the colors found in the *Haworthia cooperi cummingii*. The design on the side of the pot mimics the shape of the succulent as well. There is a nice contrast between the rounded form of the plant and the square shape of the pot. The top dressing provides separation between the pot and the succulent.

This *Aloe* 'Pink Blush' has tones of complementary colors blue and orange in its leaves. The bowl in which it is placed shares these colors. The top dressing has much more muted blues and oranges that provide a nice backdrop to make the plant stand out. The round shape of the bowl is a great contrast to the sharp, pointed leaves of the *Aloe*.

This combination of plants creates a monochromatic color scheme. The white of the pot repeats the white in the *Euphorbia polygona* 'Snowflake.' The black top dressing also repeats the black from the *Euphorbia. Rhipsalis cereusculai*, along with the two *Haworthia* varieties, adds a pop of green. The *Haworthia fasciata* repeats the white from the *Euphorbia* and the pot.

White and cool greens are the main colors in this arrangement. The shapes of the *Kalanchoe tomentosa* 'Panda Plant' and *Opuntia microdasys albata* 'Angel Wings' mimic the rounded shapes on the outside of the pot. The *Gasteria* repeats the spots of white on the *Opuntia*.

The plants in this arrangement all require similar amounts of water and sunlight. The *Aloe nobilis* mimics the height of the *Euphorbia tirucalli* and the shape of the *Echeveria agavoides*. The arrangement has a nice contrast of colors with reds and greens. The pot is a neutral color that allows the plants to take center stage.

Graptoveria 'Fred Ives' has a deep pink color, which is also found in the glaze of the pot. The stems of the *Portulacaria afra variegata* share this pink color. The greens are repeated in the *Crassula arborescens undulatifolia* and the pot. The variegation in the *Portulacaria* emphasizes the variation in colors in the pot.

These three plant varieties all do well indoors. They have similar water and sunlight needs. The repetition in pointed leaf shapes contrasts with the smooth glaze and round shape of the pot. The *Kalanchoe tomentosa* 'Panda Plant' has blue tones that coordinate with the pot, while the *Haworthias* bring out the green in the *Kalanchoe* and create an analogous color scheme.

The gold coloring of the *Mammillaria elongata,* along with the orange tones of the *Sedum adolphii,* complement the blues in the pot and *Sedum rupestre* nicely. *Sedum rupestre* repeats the shape and height of the *Mammillaria elongata* to create balance, while the *Sedum adolphii* provides a contrast in shape and height. The square pot contrasts with the mostly rounded forms in the succulents.

DISPLAYING SUCCULENTS

Succulents make a great addition to any home. Once you've found and potted the right plants for you, it's time to show them off. Find the perfect spot in your home for your plants and use some of these ideas to really get your arrangement noticed!

CONSIDER THE ROOM

A fun way to show off your succulents is by planting them in a container that goes along with the room in which they're displayed. Try planting succulents in a colander and keep it on the kitchen table. If you live in a small space, put your succulents up on a shelf on the wall.

PLAN FOR WATER RUNOFF

You've made a great choice and selected pots with a drainage hole. But even an hour or two after watering, you may still have some water drip out the bottom of the pot. Place your succulents on coasters or on a tray. This adds some visual interest and also prevents your shelf or ottoman from getting wet.

GROUPINGS

If you have a few smaller arrangements, try grouping them together for extra impact. Whether they are on a shelf or windowsill, you'll love the way they look together. Use coordinating or matching pots to get a more unified look.

GIVE THEM HEIGHT

While placing succulents on a table or windowsill looks great, add even more visual interest by giving your succulents extra height. Try displaying them on a decorative plant stand. You can also set small arrangements on a candlestick to really make them stand out.

4

SUCCULENT PROJECTS

〰〰〰〰〰〰〰〰〰

You've seen how exciting it can be to plant succulents in containers. Now comes even more fun: showcasing succulents in unique and stunning projects. Whether you're decorating for a holiday or planning a wedding, succulents will be an unepected and lovely addition. This section includes 12 beautiful succulent projects, beginning with a simple potted succulent and progressing to more complicated items, like a wreath and bouquet. While some of these projects will last for only a couple days or weeks, some can last for several years if they're maintained well.

CUTTINGS OR PLUGS?

As you prepare to create a project with succulents, one of the first things you'll need to decide is whether you want to use cuttings or plugs. How do you know which you should use?

CUTTINGS

A cutting is a succulent that has been cut off from the main plant. For the purpose of this section, a cutting does not have roots.

Benefits of Cuttings

The lack of roots makes succulent cuttings easy to work with for projects. They can easily be moved around and inserted into small spaces.

Disadvantages of Cuttings

While not having roots makes cuttings great to work with, it can also be a challenge. Before the roots form, the cuttings will shrink slightly as they take nutrients from the leaves. For this reason, you'll want to pack arrangements extra full with cuttings. It will take several weeks for the roots to fully develop and for the plant to get back to its original plump size.

Cuttings also need to be secured because they don't have roots to hold them in place initially. You'll need to use greening pins or glue to secure them, especially if the arrangement will be hanging or vertical. It is not as much of a problem when using cuttings in a pot that will maintain the same orientation as when you created it.

Finally, cuttings generally have a short stem, so it is difficult to give them extra height. You can place them on a mound of soil or use wire to give them a longer stem. Unless you are using a variety of sizes, though, it may be difficult to get very much variation in height with cuttings.

PLUGS

A plug is a succulent that has roots. This could be a full plant you just purchased with a large root ball, a cutting you took several weeks ago that now has roots, or something in between.

Benefits of Plugs

Working with rooted succulents allows projects to become established more quickly. Even a short-term project, such as a table arrangement, will look better longer when the succulents have roots so they can absorb water. Without soil, you can water the roots and keep the plants looking fresh for weeks without very much shrinkage.

Another advantage of working with plugs is that they give extra height or support to the plant, which creates more variety in an arrangement. Especially when designing in a container, plugs keep the arrangement much more secure without using anything extra. You'll still need to use greening pins for something like a wreath if you are planning on hanging it up right away. However, if you use plugs in a wreath you won't have to wait as long for the roots to be established.

Disadvantages of Plugs

One difficulty when working with plugs is getting all the roots covered. Some succulents have thick, tubular roots that are hard to move or bend without breaking. You can break the roots and the plants will still survive; however, you'll want to avoid watering them for a few days to prevent root rot.

the choice is yours

The debate between succulents and plugs is more a matter of preference. There isn't a right or wrong option. But if you have a choice, you may want to consider some of the benefits of one versus the other. The projects in this section can be made with either cuttings or plugs; feel free to use whichever you prefer.

WORKING WITH GLUE

When creating fun projects with succulents, especially when working with cuttings, it can be tricky to get them to stay in place. There are a variety of options for securing your succulents, but the most convenient and effective is often a hot glue gun.

IS IT SAFE FOR MY SUCCULENTS?

It might seem a little odd, but a hot glue gun doesn't bother succulents too much. They will burn where they touch the glue, but it doesn't affect the rest of the plant. They continue to grow and put off roots as if nothing happened! Using hot glue is much faster and cheaper than most other options and secures them quite well.

WHERE TO GLUE

While succulents can tolerate glue anywhere, the least noticeable and most effective place to use the glue is on the side of the stem near the bottom. This allows you to place the succulent in the spot you've created in your arrangement and it will adhere nicely to the moss. You can use glue on a leaf of your succulent, but if the leaf falls off or dies before the roots are strong enough, your succulent will no longer be attached to the arrangement.

WHAT TEMPERATURE IS BEST?

You can use either a high- or low-temperature glue gun. Both work equally well. A high-temp gun will burn the succulent a little bit more, but it really doesn't bother the plant. A lower-temp gun will cool faster so you don't have to hold the succulent in place as long. If you are purchasing a glue gun for your succulent projects, I'd recommend a low-temp gun.

clear tacky glue

floral glue

greening pins

ALTERNATIVES TO HOT GLUE

If you'd rather not work with hot glue, there are a few other options for attaching succulents to topiaries and other arrangements. You can use greening pins, which can be placed through the stem of the succulent and into the plant. These work well if you're using a deep moss form.

Floral glue is a great option as well. Floral glue dries in about 30 seconds and sometimes less. Unlike hot glue, it does not dry clear. It has a greenish-brown coloring that will blend in well on a moss form, but will be more noticeable on something like a napkin ring. It does tend to adhere better to the succulent than hot glue, which also means you can't rearrange once the glue has set. Floral glue is also quite expensive.

You can also use clear tacky glue. While this glue holds well, it takes a long time (two to three hours) to dry. If your arrangement is flat while you're working on it, this can be a good option. It also allows you to rearrange fairly easily because the glue doesn't set quickly. Watch out for drips on the surface below your arrangement if you use this glue.

HOW LONG WILL
MY CREATION LIVE?

The lifespan of your succulent creation will vary quite a bit based on the type of project, the climate in which you live, and the varieties of succulents used. Some projects are meant to be temporary, but you can plant the succulents in a traditional container later and they'll grow for years.

TYPE OF PROJECT

Some of the projects in this section are designed to be temporary, while others will grow and be healthy for a long time with proper care. Projects such as the Succulent-Topped Pumpkin, Long Table Centerpiece, Decorated Napkin Ring, Boutonnière, and Bouquet will generally last only a few days before they need attention and a more permanent container. The great thing is you can easily plant them in a pot when you are finished with your event. This is a great way for a bride to have something from her wedding for years to come.

Most of the other projects will generally grow for several years if they are maintained well. The Glass Terrarium will likely last for a few months before it shrivels up from lack of water or rots from too much, unless you add a drainage hole. You'll need to maintain and care for your projects like you would a traditional potted arrangement. Make sure your succulents are getting the water, sunlight, and nutrients they need.

ENVIRONMENT AND CARE

Some of the temporary arrangements can be maintained for several days and even weeks if you give them extra attention. Your climate also has a big impact on how long they will live. In a slightly humid environment succulents can absorb water from the air, which helps to increase their longevity. You can also mist them from time to time to encourage some root growth. This will keep the succulents alive longer, but they won't necessarily look as pretty as they did originally.

SUCCULENT VARIETY

If you use thicker-leaved succulents in your temporary projects, they will be able to survive much longer than thinner-leaved succulents. *Echeverias* are a great example of succulents that can last for several days and even weeks without water. On the other hand, something like *Portulacaria afra* or *Crassula arborescens undulatifolia* will shrivel and die within two to four days in most places.

how long did the bouquet last?

The succulent bouquet created for this book used a variety of succulents. The *Graptosedum* 'California Sunset' lasted for about four weeks before looking really wilted. Most of the other succulents didn't last as long. The *Senecio haworthii* lasted only about three days before starting to shrivel, and by the end of the week they were completely dried up.

TERRA COTTA OR CERAMIC POT

The best place to start when working with succulents is with a terra cotta or ceramic pot arrangement. While the principles are basic, such an arrangement can be the perfect accent to your front porch, table, or mantle. The options and combinations are endless! You could use a large pot, small pot, colorful succulents, green succulents, tall plants, short plants, etc. The hardest part will be deciding what you want to use. However, you'll likely find that designing with succulents is easier than you thought.

MATERIALS

- **Succulents**
  (1 thriller, 1 spiller,
  and 2 to 3 filler varieties)
- **Pot**
- **Hot glue gun**
- **Wire mesh**
- **Soil**
- **Top dressing**

1. Place a small piece of mesh over the opening in the bottom of the pot.

2. To prevent the mesh from moving, secure it using hot glue.

3. Fill the pot with a succulent soil mix. Mound the soil slightly in the center of the pot.

4. Begin by placing your "thriller" succulent at the top of the mound. Bury the roots, if any, in the soil.

5 Add the "spiller" succulents along the edges and use "filler" succulents to keep them in place.

6 Finish adding in the "filler" succulents.

7 You may find that as you add in the "filler" succulents, the plants will need to be re-arranged to fit together and look balanced.

8 Add a top dressing to finish off the arrangement.

STRAWBERRY POT

If you're looking for something a little different than the typical ceramic pot, try a strawberry pot! These pots come in a variety of sizes and colors and have "pockets" poking out of the sides. Not only do you have plants at the top, but along the sides of the planter as well. Succulents work well in these pockets because they don't need a lot of space for roots. This planter is a simple way to add interest to your succulent garden.

MATERIALS

- **Planter**
- **Succulents** (3 to 5 varieties)
- **Saw or pipe cutter** (not pictured)
- **Drill** with ⅟₁₆-inch (1.5mm) drill bit
- **PVC pipe** (1-inch; 2.5cm diameter)
- **Wire mesh**
- **Duct tape**
- **Soil**

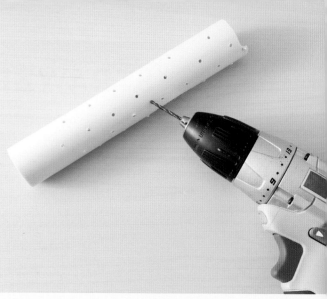

1 Using a saw or pipe cutter, cut a piece of PVC pipe just taller than your strawberry pot.

2 Drill ¹⁄₁₆-inch (1.5mm) holes all along the pipe about 1 inch (2.5cm) apart. Leave 1 to 2 inches (2.5–5cm) at the top of the pipe without holes.

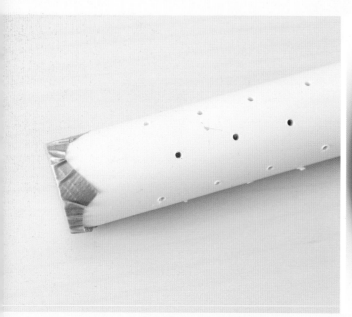

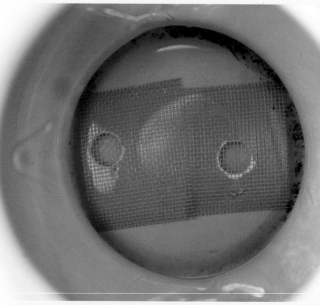

3 Place duct tape over the top end of the pipe. This will prevent soil from getting in as you fill the planter.

4 Place wire mesh over the holes in the bottom of the strawberry planter to prevent soil from coming out.

5 Place the PVC pipe in the center of the pot.

6 Fill the bottom of the planter with soil until it reaches the lowest pocket in the strawberry planter.

7 Add your succulents to the lower pocket, starting with any hanging succulents.

8 Once you like the arrangement, fill the inside of the pot with soil until it reaches the bottom of the next pocket, then add succulents to the pocket.

9 Continue adding soil and succulents until all the pockets are filled. Make sure to keep the PVC pipe centered.

10 When you reach the top of the planter, add larger succulents to the top around the PVC pipe.

11 Arrange the succulents so the top of the pipe is concealed, but leave it accessible so that you can water the planter through the pipe.

12 Add a top dressing to the top of the pot and to the pockets if desired. Remove duct tape from the top of the PVC pipe.

13 To water the planter, pour water into the pipe. This helps distribute the water evenly throughout the planter.

14 Be sure to keep the planter in an area that gets plenty of light, and rotate it from time to time so that all the succulents get enough light.

HANGING PLANTER

A hanging planter is a simple but unique way to display succulents. While a potted arrangement is usually viewed from above, a hanging arrangement is viewed from below or at eye level. Focus on height and depth when designing a hanging arrangement. Trailing succulents will really make this planter exciting and beautiful. You'll also want taller succulents that will show above the rim of the planter when it's hanging. Have fun combining a variety of plants to create a stunning arrangement!

MATERIALS

- **Hanging planter**
- **Coconut liner**
- **Succulents** (3 to 5 varieties)
- **Medium decorative rocks** (optional)
- **Soil**
- **Top dressing**

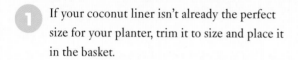

1 If your coconut liner isn't already the perfect size for your planter, trim it to size and place it in the basket.

2 Fill the basket about three-quarters full with soil.

3 Place the trailing succulents first. Insert the end of the cutting under the soil to hold the plant in place.

4 Use a variety of trailing succulents for extra interest and to add contrast to the arrangement.

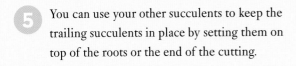

5 You can use your other succulents to keep the trailing succulents in place by setting them on top of the roots or the end of the cutting.

6 If the other succulents aren't strong enough to hold the hanging succulents in place, place a rock over the roots to secure the plants.

7 Add your tallest succulents to the arrangement near the center.

8 Fill the planter the rest of the way with soil so all the roots are covered.

9 Finish adding succulents to fill in the planter.

10 Once you like the arrangement, add your top dressing.

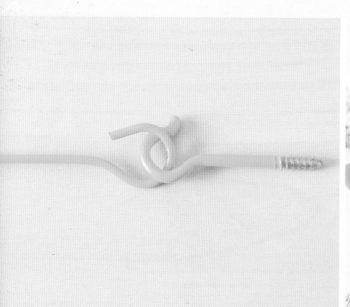

11 Your planter can be hung once you've finished the arrangement. Be sure it is tightly secured so it doesn't fall.

12 If your arrangement will be kept inside, take it down to water. Water thoroughly when the soil is dry.

BIRDCAGE

There's something whimsical and fun about succulents in a birdcage. The way they peek out between the bars and hang below the base is enchanting. If you hang your birdcage, it also makes for a great variation on a hanging planter. You can fill your entire birdcage with succulents, create a fairy garden in the middle, or do something in between. As the succulents grow, your birdcage will fill up more and more. The tight groupings of succulents will look gorgeous with the metal bars to frame them.

MATERIALS

- **Birdcage** (make sure it opens from the top so you can fit succulents inside)
- **Succulents** (3 to 5 varieties)
- **Drill** with 1/16-inch (1.5mm) drill bit (or a hammer and nail)
- **Sphagnum moss**
- **Soil**
- **Gravel**

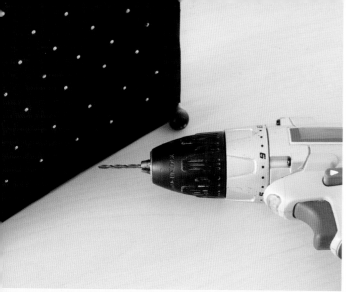

1 Drill holes in the bottom of the birdcage for drainage.

2 Cover the bottom of the birdcage with gravel to weigh it down. This will help prevent it from tipping over if it is sitting rather than hanging.

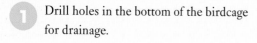

3 Soak the sphagnum moss with water.

4 Create a thick lining of sphagnum moss along the edges of the birdcage.

5 Fill the bottom of the birdcage with soil.

6 Begin adding succulents, starting from the bottom with trailing succulents.

7 Use your fingers to make holes in the moss along the bottom and sides of the birdcage.

8 Insert succulents into the holes you've made in the sphagnum moss.

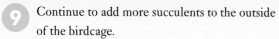

9 Continue to add more succulents to the outside of the birdcage.

10 Add succulents to the inside of the birdcage, starting with the largest plants.

11 Fill the inside with more soil to reach the top of the moss lining.

12 As you add succulents to the inside of the birdcage, allow some to stick out between the bars.

13 Finish filling in the interior of the birdcage with succulents.

14 Close the top and arrange taller succulents so they fit through the bars.

15 Care for your birdcage as you would a container arrangement. If you are using a metal birdcage, keep it out of direct afternoon sunlight, as this can cause the metal to heat up and burn the plants.

GLASS TERRARIUM

There's something intriguing about planting in glass. A terrarium is its own little world in a clear container, allowing you to see in. You can select a variety of colors for rocks and pebbles to add to the bottom of the bowl, or leave it looking more natural with just the soil and neutral rocks. An interesting technique is to use succulents that resemble coral for an under-the-sea look with seashells on top of the soil. Whatever you choose, a terrarium adds charm to any space.

MATERIALS

- **Succulents** (1 large, 2 to 4 smaller varieties)
- **Glass bowl**
- **Diatomaceous earth**
- **Coconut coir**
- **Large decorative rock**
- **Small decorative rocks** (top dressing)
- **Moss** (a few clumps)

selecting your bowl

One of the more crucial parts of creating a terrarium with succulents is finding a bowl that will allow the succulents to live as long as possible. It's best to select a shallow bowl with a wide opening. This allows plenty of air flow and makes it easier for the pooled water to evaporate.

If you're feeling ambitious and you want your terrarium to last more than a few weeks, drill a hole in the bottom of the bowl with a diamond-tipped drill bit to allow drainage. You'll still need to be careful not to overwater, but this will keep your succulents healthy much longer.

1. Spread about 1 inch (2.5cm) of diatomaceous earth in the bottom of the bowl.

2. Spread a layer of coconut coir over the top of the diatomaceous earth, about ½ inch (1.25cm) thick.

3. Be sure not to mix the coir with the diatomaceous earth so that they appear as separate layers.

4. Spread half of your small rocks on top of the coconut coir.

5 Place your largest succulent in the bowl first. Add a little bit more soil to cover the roots.

6 Place the large decorative rock. If needed, this can help hold the larger succulent in place.

7 Fill in with the rest of the succulents and cover the roots with soil.

8 A terrarium tends to look best if the succulents are grouped together rather than spread out.

9 Add the other rocks to the bowl and use them to cover any roots.

10 Tuck clumps of moss around the succulents and rocks to create a finished look.

11 Place your terrarium in a spot that gets plenty of sunlight.

12 Water the terrarium when the soil dries out by pouring a measured amount of water, about half the volume of your soil, on top.

SUCCULENT-TOPPED PUMPKIN

*Give your autumn décor an unexpected twist with this festive succulent-topped
pumpkin. It's a unique—and less messy—alternative to the traditional carved pumpkin.
Try pairing your succulents with pumpkins of different shapes, sizes, and colors.
A smaller pumpkin will make a colorful centerpiece for your Thanksgiving table, while
a larger pumpkin will bring seasonal color and interest to your front porch.*

MATERIALS

- **Pumpkin**
- **Succulent cuttings**
  (3 to 5 smaller varieties)
- **Sphagnum moss**
- **Spray adhesive**
- **Glue gun**
- **Sharp knife**
- **Fall accents**

① Cut off the stem of the pumpkin so it is almost flush with the top.

② Spray adhesive generously on the top of the pumpkin.

③ Attach dry sphagnum moss where you sprayed the adhesive. Use more adhesive if necessary to get the moss as you'd like it.

④ Once the moss is just right, begin attaching succulents.

5 Start from the center and work your way out.

6 Use hot glue to hold the succulents in place.

7 The hot glue will not adhere to the pumpkin, so make sure your succulent is on the moss.

8 Place taller succulents in the center and use shorter succulents around them.

9 Add other seasonal objects such as acorns or pine-cones as desired.

10 Use hanging succulents along the outer edge of the pumpkin top for extra visual interest.

11 Keep the succulent-topped pumpkin looking great by misting it with water every few days, soaking the moss as much as possible.

12 Be sure to provide several hours of morning sun to the pumpkin to help the succulents maintain their shape and color.

reuse your succulents

The pumpkin can last for several weeks, until the pumpkin itself begins to get soggy. You can then remove the succulents and use them in your garden or for another project.

LIVING PICTURE

There's something appealing about plants growing vertically rather than in a pot. Succulents do especially well in vertical arrangements, so they are a popular choice for creating living pictures. A living picture can cover an entire wall, or it can be something smaller and more personal. If you're growing indoors, small and personal is a great option. Find a color palette of succulents that you like, or choose a variety of shapes and textures. Rosettes are a popular choice for living pictures, but branchy, trailing, and even somewhat tall succulents work well too.

MATERIALS

- **Wood shadowbox frame**
- **Soil**
- **Succulent cuttings** (3 to 5 varieties)
- **Sphagnum moss**
- **Pencil or wooden craft stick**

1 Fill the frame with soil up to the wire.

2 Soak the sphagnum moss with water.

3 Spread a layer of sphagnum moss over the soil in the frame opening.

4 Remove the lower leaves on the succulent cuttings, creating about 1 to 2 inches (2.5–5cm) of bare stem.

5 Use a pencil or wooden craft stick to create a hole in the moss and soil.

6 Insert the succulent cutting into the hole.

7 Using this method, create waves of succulents by placing several of the same succulent type in a diagonal or curved line.

8 If desired, add a larger succulent to the frame to create a focal point.

9 Use branchy or trailing succulents to add visual interest along the edge of the frame.

10 Continue to fill the frame with succulents. Keep the succulents close together because they will shrink slightly before growing.

11 Fill any gaps with clumps of moss.

12 Leave the frame horizontal for 6 to 8 weeks until the succulents have fully taken root. It makes a great table decoration!

13 Once your cuttings have rooted, hang the living picture or stand it up on a shelf.

14 To water the living picture, remove it from the wall and pour water on top, completely soaking the soil. Water your living picture weekly or when the soil dries out.

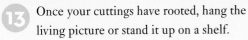

drainage

If your frame doesn't have drainage holes, consider drilling holes in
what will be the bottom of the picture so water can easily drain out.
When lying flat, water should be able to seep out the back of the frame.
When standing, water can drain out the front of the arrangement,
but it will last longer if there are drainage holes in the frame.

LONG TABLE CENTERPIECE

Succulents can last several days without being watered and still look fabulous. For this reason, they make a great table centerpiece for any event. There are a variety of ways you could create a centerpiece: a long box full of succulents, a grouping of potted succulents, or unpotted succulents on the table. This last option creates a very organic look that works well with any décor. The rocks and succulents you choose will greatly impact the style of your centerpiece.

MATERIALS

- **Succulents**
  (3 to 5 varieties, including a trailing succulent similar to *Senecio radicans*)

- **Sphagnum moss**
- **Burlap table runner**
- **Plastic wrap**
- **Large decorative rocks**

- **Small decorative rocks**
- **Scissors** (not pictured)
- **Masking tape** (not pictured)

1. Spread out a layer or two of plastic wrap where your table runner and centerpiece will be placed. Tape the ends under the table with masking tape to hold it in place.

2. Lay the burlap table runner across the table, covering the plastic wrap.

3. If the plastic wrap is too wide, fold the edges under so they are covered by the burlap.

4. Trim the ends of the table runner to the desired length. Cut each end to come to a point in the center.

5 On the center of the runner, spread a handful or two of small decorative rocks.

6 Place larger decorative rocks randomly among the smaller rocks.

7 Add a small patch of sphagnum moss on top of the rocks near the center.

8 Place a large succulent in the center of the moss and rocks.

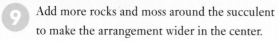

9 Add more rocks and moss around the succulent to make the arrangement wider in the center.

10 Add a few smaller succulents around the large succulent to create a small grouping. This will tie in the large succulent with the smaller groupings.

11 Group smaller succulents along the rocks in several places.

12 If needed, use the larger rocks and moss to help succulents stand up.

13 Cover any visible roots with clumps of moss.

14 Place several strands of trailing succulents around the smaller succulents. Hide the ends under the other succulents.

15 Create additional groupings of rocks, moss, and succulents along the table runner. The total number of groupings should be an odd number, such as 3 or 5.

16 To maintain the arrangement for several days, spray the bottom of the arrangements with water every other day. The plastic wrap will prevent the water from damaging the table.

SUCCULENT WREATH

A succulent wreath makes a great addition to any door, room, or wall. Even though it's living, you'll find it is easy to maintain and doesn't require much attention. The types of succulents you choose will have a large impact on the look and style of your wreath. You can combine a variety of brightly colored succulents in a range of shapes and textures for a bold look, or select succulents of similar colors and textures to create a more uniform piece. Either way, a succulent wreath is sure to be an impressive addition to your décor.

MATERIALS

- **Succulent cuttings**
  (about 100)
- **Wire wreath frame**
  (15 inches; 38cm)
- **Wire**

- **Wire cutters**
- **Sphagnum moss**
  (approx. 100 cubic
  inches; 1,640cc)
- **Clear fishing line**

- **Scissors**
- **Greening pins**
- **Hot glue gun**
- **Wooden craft stick
  or pencil**

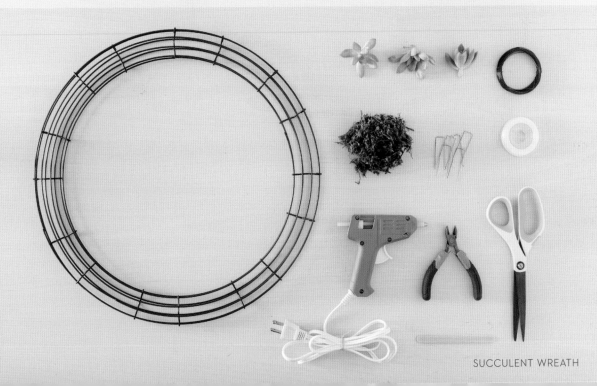

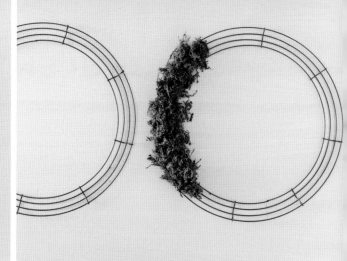

1 Soak the sphagnum moss in water. This will make it easy to work with in the wreath form. If used dry, it creates a mess and doesn't work well.

2 Your wire frame should have two pieces: a top and bottom (although they may look the same). Open the wire wreath frame and begin filling the bottom piece with sphagnum moss.

3 Once the bottom piece is filled with moss, place the top on the wreath form. Cut short pieces of wire and wrap them around the wreath form to secure the two pieces together.

4 Once the wreath form is secure, continue to stuff the form with moss. You'll want to pack the moss in tightly because it compresses when it dries, so the more the better.

5   After you've stuffed the wreath form, wrap fishing line around the form to keep the moss in place. Wrap the fishing line around several times to make sure the moss is secure.

6   Before you begin adding succulents to your frame, lay them out on the table as you plan to arrange them on the wreath. Play with the arrangement until you're happy with the design.

7   To add succulents to the wreath, poke the wooden craft stick or pencil into the moss and wiggle it around to make a hole.

8   Insert the stem of your succulent cutting into the hole. Secure the cutting with hot glue, a greening pin, or both.

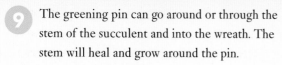

9 The greening pin can go around or through the stem of the succulent and into the wreath. The stem will heal and grow around the pin.

10 You can also place the greening pin over the leaf of the succulent to hold the cutting in place. This does less damage to the succulent but is not as secure because the leaf may fall off.

11 Hot glue can be used in addition to or in place of the greening pins. Place a small amount on the stem and then insert the stem into the hole you created in the wreath.

12 Continue to create holes in the wreath and add your succulent cuttings. Make sure to keep the cuttings close together because they shrink slightly before growing.

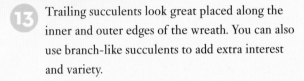

13 Trailing succulents look great placed along the inner and outer edges of the wreath. You can also use branch-like succulents to add extra interest and variety.

14 Once your wreath is finished, allow it to lay flat and dry for 4 to 6 weeks until the cuttings have rooted. Keep it in an area with a mild temperature and indirect sunlight.

15 When your cuttings have rooted, hang up the wreath and enjoy!

16 To care for the wreath, allow it to dry out almost completely before watering and then soak thoroughly. Laying the wreath on the lawn when the sprinklers are running is a great way to do this.

DECORATED NAPKIN RING

What better way to dress up a table setting than with succulents? Whether you're planning an event or just want to make dinner a little more special, these simple succulent-decorated napkin rings will add a touch of elegance. This tutorial shows you how to create your own napkin ring using wire and floral tape, but you can also decorate a premade wooden ring. Both options are easy to do and look great.

MATERIALS

- **Succulent cuttings** (3 to 5 per ring)
- **Floral wire**
- **Floral tape**
- **Wire cutters**
- **Scissors**
- **Ribbon**
- **Hot glue gun**
- **Wooden napkin ring** (optional)

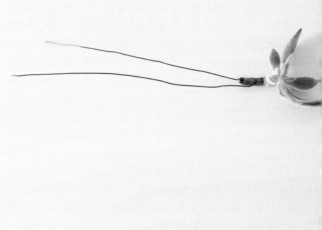

1 Remove the lower leaves from the succulent cuttings.

2 Cut a piece of wire about 1 foot (30.5cm) long, insert it through the stem, and bend it in half.

3 Twist the wire together. This strengthens and elongates the stem.

4 Wrap floral tape around the wire. Stretching the tape slightly makes it sticky, so it adheres to itself.

5 Create a long stem for each of the succulents you are using by repeating steps 2 through 4.

6 Align 3 to 5 succulents and cross the wire stems.

7 Use floral tape to secure two of the larger succulents together.

8 Add the rest of the succulents and secure them with floral tape.

9 Twist the wires together and then loop them in a circle.

10 Cover the loop with floral tape (and more wire if needed) to secure it.

11 Tie the ribbon to the top of the ring near the succulents.

12 Wrap the loop with ribbon.

13 Loop the ribbon between the succulents to cover any floral tape.

14 Tie off with a bow or use hot glue to secure it.

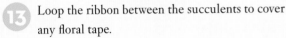

wooden napkin ring

Another option for creating a napkin ring with succulents is to use a premade wooden napkin ring and hot glue succulents on top. If you do this, try using a few hanging succulents with a larger succulent in the center. Be sure to cut the stem of the main succulent extremely short so that it sits almost flush with the wooden ring. You can also attach ribbon with the hot glue before adding the succulents.

SUCCULENT BOUTONNIÈRE

Succulents work extremely well for boutonnières. They're sturdier than most flowers and won't wilt as quickly. With their wide variety of shapes, sizes, and colors, you can find succulents to work with any style of wedding, whether it's modern, rustic, classic, or vintage. This boutonnière tutorial uses only succulents, but you could mix in some flowers for added color and texture.

MATERIALS

- Succulent cuttings
  (1 to 3 per boutonnière)
- Floral wire
- Wire cutters
- Floral tape
- Scissors
- Ribbon or twine
- Decorative pins

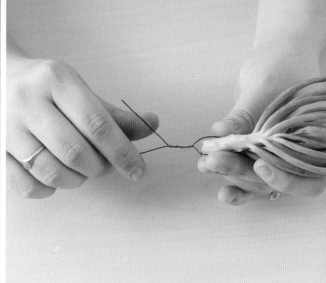

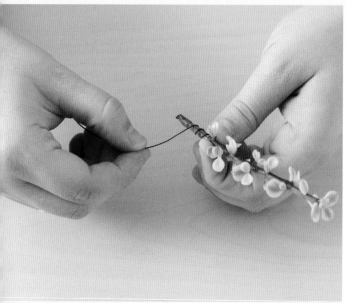

1 Remove any extra leaves from the stem.

2 Cut a short piece of wire, insert it through the stem, and bend it in half. Twist the wire together. This strengthens and elongates the stem.

3 Alternatively, you can wrap wire around the stem several times.

4 Wrap floral tape around the wire. Stretching the tape slightly will make it sticky, so it can stick to itself.

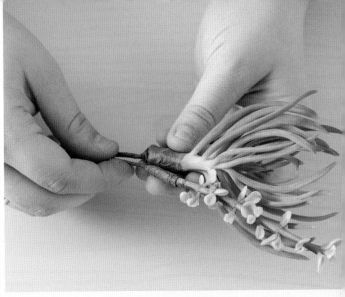

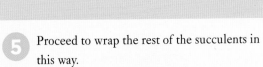
5 Proceed to wrap the rest of the succulents in this way.

6 Arrange the succulents by holding onto the stems.

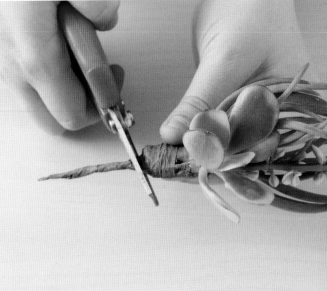

7 Wrap all the succulents together with floral tape.

8 Trim off any excess wire on the end.

9 Use a coordinating ribbon or twine to wrap around the stems.

10 Tie a knot to secure the ribbon. Trim the ends of the ribbon to the desired length.

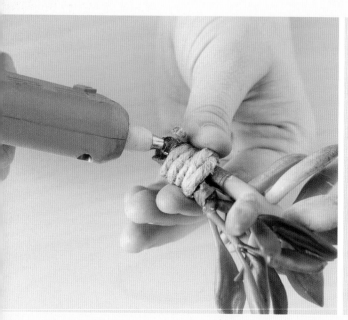

11 Use hot glue to secure the end of the ribbon if you don't want to tie a knot.

12 Insert a pin to use for securing on a lapel.

after the event

The succulents in the boutonnière will generally last for several days without looking wilted. A mild, slightly humid environment will keep them looking fresh longer. After your event, you can pull out the succulents and plant them as you would normal cuttings.

BOUQUET

If you're looking for a really incredible succulent project, this is it: the succulent bouquet. Working with succulents in bouquets is a great way to add variety and texture. Plus, the bride or bridesmaids will have a keepsake at the end of the day. They can plant the succulents and have something to remember the wedding by for years to come. Creating a bouquet with only succulents can be a bit tricky, but it's well worth it. Nothing can beat a gorgeous arrangement of succulents on a special day.

MATERIALS

- **Succulent cuttings**
  (20 to 30 in 5 to 7 varieties)
- **Floral wire**
- **Wire cutters**

- **Floral tape**
- **Scissors**
- **Wooden skewers**
  (for heavy succulents)

- **Ribbon**
  (1- to 2-inches
  [2.5–5cm] wide)
- **Decorative pins**

1. Remove any unwanted lower leaves from your succulents.

2. Cut a piece of wire about 2 feet (.6m) long. Insert the wire through the stem of a succulent cutting.

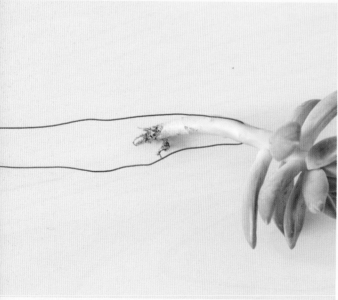

3. Pull the wire until there is an even amount on each side, then bend the wire downward.

4. Wrap the wire, beginning at the succulent stem, with floral tape.

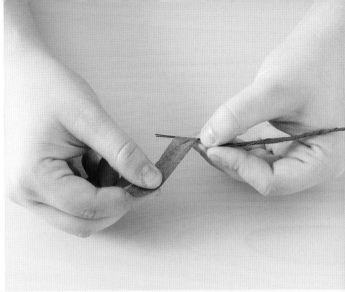

5 Be sure to stretch the tape slightly as you go. This causes the tape to become tacky and stick to itself.

6 Once the wire is covered with tape, cut the tape and finish wrapping the end.

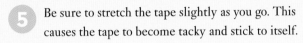

7 Repeat this process with each succulent you are using.

8 For larger succulents, you can use a wood skewer and wire to keep the succulent more stable.

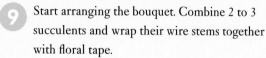

9 Start arranging the bouquet. Combine 2 to 3 succulents and wrap their wire stems together with floral tape.

10 Look for shapes that fit together when combining the different pieces. Succulents are not as flexible as flowers, so it's important to make sure they fit together well.

11 Tape the stems together as you go to keep them in place. This makes it easier to add other stems without losing the shape you've created.

12 The bases don't all need to align at the bottom. Vary the heights of the succulents to create visual interest.

13 Once you have all the flowers combined, secure them again with floral tape so the whole bouquet is one piece.

14 Trim the ends so they are all the same length.

15 Use a long ribbon to cover the wire stems. Start and the bottom and work upward. Overlap the edges to ensure the stems are not visible.

16 Tie a bow to secure the ribbon or use decorative pins.

5

SUCCULENT VARIETIES

~~~~~~~~~~~~~~~~~~~~~~~~~

There are so many succulents to choose from that it can be overwhelming. Plus, the various genera and species of succulents have a surprisingly wide spread of needs when it comes to light, water, and temperature. You'll often choose different succulents for growing in the ground outdoors than you would for a container indoors. Some succulents are sensitive to overwatering, while others need to be watered frequently. You'll need full sun for some succulents to thrive, whereas others like cool shade. This section highlights 100 succulent varieties and details their specific needs.

Adromischus cristatus

CRINKLE-LEAF PLANT

This easy-to-care-for plant has an unusual shape on the ends of its leaves. When it's getting too much sun, the leaves move to one side of the plant, away from the harsh light. It also propagates easily from leaf cuttings.

MATURE SIZE

18 inches
(45 cm)

WATER

Average

SUN

Full sun,
partial shade

HARDINESS

Zone 9b
25°F (−3.8°C)

PAIRS WITH

Graptosedum
'California
Sunset'

Adromischus maculatus

This succulent has purple spotting that gives it a unique color. It works well for adding variety to an arrangement.

MATURE SIZE
6 inches
(15.25 cm)

WATER
Average

SUN
Full sun,
light shade,
partial shade

HARDINESS
Zone 9b
25°F (−3.8°C)

PAIRS WITH
Sempervivum
'Pacific Devil's Food'

Aeonium
'Kiwi'

Aeonium 'Kiwi' has beautiful green and yellow rosettes with a tinge of pink along the edges. It propagates easily from cuttings.

MATURE SIZE

12 inches
(30 cm)

WATER

Average

SUN

Full sun,
light shade,
partial shade

HARDINESS

Zone 9b
25°F (−3.8°C)

PAIRS WITH

Crassula arborescens undulatifolia

Aeonium 'Sunburst'

Aeonium 'Sunburst' grows easily in most climates and tends to do well indoors. It can easily sunburn, so avoid placing in an area with hot, direct sunlight.

MATURE SIZE

18 inches
(45 cm)

WATER

Above
average

SUN

Full sun,
partial shade

HARDINESS

Zone 9b
25°F (−3.8°C)

PAIRS WITH

*Aeonium
arboretum*
'Zwartkop'

Aeonium arboreum 'Zwartkop'

BLACK TREE AEONIUM,
PURPLE CREST AEONIUM

Aeonium arboretum 'Zwartkop' provides a nice contrast to many lighter-colored plants. It grows well in pots and can become bushy when planted in an outdoor garden.

MATURE SIZE

48 inches
(120 cm)

WATER

Above
average

SUN

Full sun

HARDINESS

Zone 9b
25°F (−3.8°C)

PAIRS WITH

Aloe juvenna

Aloe
'Black Beauty'

This dark green *Aloe* is a great plant for growing in containers. It offsets easily, so you'll quickly have more plants.

MATURE SIZE
12 inches
(30 cm)

WATER
Average

SUN
Full sun,
light shade,
partial shade

HARDINESS
Zone 9b
25°F (−3.8°C)

PAIRS WITH
*Euphorbia
polygona*
'Snowflake'

Aloe brevifolia

SHORT-LEAVED ALOE

This clumping *Aloe* is great for beginners. It grows well in containers and can tolerate some overwatering.

MATURE SIZE
6 inches
(15 cm)

WATER
Average

SUN
Full sun

HARDINESS
Zone 11
40°F (4.5°C)

PAIRS WITH
Crassula rupestris

Aloe
'Christmas Carol'

This is one of the more colorful *Aloes*. Its red color deepens when stressed by cold or lack of water.

MATURE SIZE
6 inches
(15 cm)

WATER
Average

SUN
Full sun,
partial shade

HARDINESS
Zone 10a
30°F (−1.1°C)

PAIRS WITH
*Mammillaria
rhodantha*

Aloe
'Crosby's Prolific'

In the sun, *Aloe* 'Crosby's Prolific' turns light pink. It is a clumping *Aloe* and grows quickly.

MATURE SIZE
6 inches
(15 cm)

WATER
Average

SUN
Full sun,
partial shade

HARDINESS
Zone 9b
25°F (−3.8°C)

PAIRS WITH
Graptoveria
'Fred Ives'

Aloe
'Doran Black'

Aloe 'Doran Black' grows well indoors. Its unique white color makes this plant a sought-after variety.

MATURE SIZE
6 inches
(15 cm)

WATER
Average

SUN
Full sun,
light shade,
partial shade

HARDINESS
Zone 10a
30°F (−1.1°C)

PAIRS WITH
Senecio rowleyanus

Aloe haworthioides

HAWORTHIA-LEAVED ALOE

The spines on this *Aloe* give it an almost fuzzy look, although the spines are quite sharp. It resembles the *Haworthia* family more than the *Aloe* family.

MATURE SIZE
12 inches
(30 cm)

WATER
Average

SUN
Full sun,
partial shade

HARDINESS
Zone 9b
25°F (−3.8°C)

PAIRS WITH
*Anacampseros
telephiastrum
variegata*

Aloe juvenna

TIGER-TOOTH ALOE

While most *Aloes* tend to stay low to the ground, *Aloe juvenna* grows in tall stacks. Like most other *Aloes*, it offsets easily.

MATURE SIZE
24 inches
(60 cm)

WATER
Average

SUN
Full sun,
partial shade

HARDINESS
Zone 9a
20°F (−6.6°C)

PAIRS WITH
Kalanchoe longiflora coccinea

Aloe nobilis

GOLD-TOOTH ALOE

Aloe nobilis grows well indoors. It forms tight rosettes and clusters easily.

MATURE SIZE

12 inches
(30 cm)

WATER

Average

SUN

Full sun,
partial shade

HARDINESS

Zone 9a
20°F (−6.6°C)

PAIRS WITH

*Mammillaria
elongata*

Aloe
'Twilight Zone'

This succulent has tiny white spines spread over each leaf rather than just along the edges. It clumps easily and makes a stunning addition to a potted arrangement.

MATURE SIZE
**12 inches
(30 cm)**

WATER
Average

SUN
**Full sun,
light shade,
partial shade**

HARDINESS
**Zone 9b
25°F (−3.8°C)**

PAIRS WITH
*Anacampseros
rufescens*

Aloe vera

MEDICINAL ALOE

Aloe vera is well known for its medicinal properties. If you break open one of its leaves, the clear gel within can be used to soothe minor cuts and burns. It grows well indoors, so it's easy to take advantage of its healing abilities.

MATURE SIZE

24 inches
(60 cm)

WATER

Below
average

SUN

Full sun,
light shade,
partial shade

HARDINESS

Zone 9a
20°F (−6.6°C)

PAIRS WITH

*Echeveria
imbricata*

Anacampseros rufescens

This small, clumping succulent is a much-sought-after plant. It spreads easily and stays low to the ground, making it a great filler for container arrangements.

MATURE SIZE

3 inches
(7.5 cm)

WATER

Average,
sensitive to
overwatering

SUN

Full sun,
partial shade,
light shade

HARDINESS

Zone 9b
25°F (−3.8°C)

PAIRS WITH

Crassula
'Tom Thumb'

Anacampseros telephiastrum variegata

This succulent is very colorful and grows well indoors. Its rosy, pink-tinged leaves lend a nice variety to container arrangements.

MATURE SIZE

3 inches
(7.5 cm)

WATER

Average,
sensitive to
overwatering

SUN

Full sun,
partial shade

HARDINESS

Zone 10b
35°F (1.7°C)

PAIRS WITH

Echeveria
'Lola'

Cephalocereus senilis

OLD MAN CACTUS, OLD MAN OF MEXICO

This fuzzy cactus is frequently sold small in nurseries but can grow up to 40 feet (12m) tall. Under the fuzzy white hair are sharp spines, so it should be handled with care.

MATURE SIZE

40 feet
(12m)

WATER

Average

SUN

Full sun

HARDINESS

Zone 9b
25°F (−3.8°C)

PAIRS WITH

*Echeveria
purpusorum*

Cereus hildmannianus uruguayanus

FAIRY CASTLE CACTUS

This cactus grows very well indoors. Its unique shape and texture makes it a sought-after specimen.

MATURE SIZE

36 inches
(90 cm)

WATER

Average

SUN

Light shade,
full shade

HARDINESS

Zone 10a
30°F (−1.1°C)

PAIRS WITH

*Faucaria
tigrina*

Ceropegia woodii variegata

ROSARY VINE, STRING OF HEARTS

Ceropegia woodii variegata has beautiful green and pink heart-shaped leaves. It grows very well indoors and works great as a "spiller" in arrangements.

MATURE SIZE
36 inches
(90 cm)

WATER
Average

SUN
Light shade

HARDINESS
Zone 11
40°F (4.5°C)

PAIRS WITH
Graptoveria
'Silver Star'

Cotyledon tomentosa ladismithensis

BEAR'S PAW

This succulent's nickname is right on; it's paw-shaped leaves even have bumpy "claws" at the edges. The tips of the leaves turn reddish-brown when they get enough sunlight.

MATURE SIZE

12 inches
(30 cm)

WATER

Average

SUN

Full sun

HARDINESS

Zone 9b
25°F (−3.8°C)

PAIRS WITH

Graptoveria
'Candle Blue'

Crassula arborescens

SILVER DOLLAR JADE

The rounded shape of the *Crassula arborescens'* leaves gives it a nice contrast to other succulents. It propagates easily from leaves and cuttings.

MATURE SIZE
6 feet
(1.8m)

WATER
Average

SUN
Full sun

HARDINESS
Zone 9b
25°F (−3.8°C)

PAIRS WITH
Echeveria harmsii

Crassula arborescens undulatifolia

RIPPLE JADE

The unusual wave of the *Crassula arborescens undulatifolia* leaves creates a great visual contrast to other succulents. The leaves develop a red edge with enough sunlight.

MATURE SIZE

36 inches
(90 cm)

WATER

Average

SUN

Full sun,
partial shade

HARDINESS

Zone 9b
25°F (−3.8°C)

PAIRS WITH

Graptoveria
'Fred Ives'

Crassula capitella

CAMPFIRE CRASSULA

In full sunlight, this plant turns deep red, giving it its fiery nickname. It clusters easily, so it will fill a container arrangement nicely.

MATURE SIZE
12 inches
(30cm)

WATER
Average

SUN
Full sun,
partial shade

HARDINESS
Zone 9b
25°F (−3.8°C)

PAIRS WITH
*Mammillaria
elongata*

Crassula falcata

PROPELLER PLANT

With leaves shaped like propellers, this succulent looks like it is about to take off! It grows in tall stems and will have a large red flower in the summer.

MATURE SIZE

18 inches (45cm)

WATER

Average, sensitive to overwatering

SUN

Full sun

HARDINESS

Zone 9b
25°F (−3.8°C)

PAIRS WITH

Senecio vitalis

Crassula marginalis rubra variegata

This *Crassula* is a great "spiller" in container arrangements. Its leaves can be either solid green or variegated.

MATURE SIZE
3 inches
(8cm)

WATER
Average

SUN
Full sun,
partial shade

HARDINESS
Zone 9b
25°F (−3.8°C)

PAIRS WITH
*Mammillaria
plumosa*

Crassula marnieriana

WORM PLANT

These little "worms" are fantastic for container arrangements. In lower light they tend to stretch out, but otherwise will stay nice and compact.

MATURE SIZE

6 inches
(15cm)

WATER

Average

SUN

Full sun,
partial shade

HARDINESS

Zone 11
40°F (4.5°C)

PAIRS WITH

*Sedum
clavatum*

Crassula muscosa

WATCH CHAIN PLANT

The tall strands of this *Crassula* are a great complement to any other succulent. It grows easily from cuttings.

MATURE SIZE
12 inches (30cm)

WATER
Average

SUN
Full sun

HARDINESS
Zone 9a 20°F (−6.6°C)

PAIRS WITH
Crassula falcata

Crassula ovata

JADE, MONEY TREE

Crassula ovata is one of the more common succulents. It grows well indoors and is easy to care for. You can easily propagate *Crassula ovata* from cuttings and leaves.

MATURE SIZE

6 feet
(1.8m)

WATER

Average

SUN

Full sun

HARDINESS

Zone 9a
20°F (−6.6°C)

PAIRS WITH

Sedum nussbaurmerianum

Crassula ovata 'Gollum'

GOLLUM JADE

The tubular shape of
its leaves makes this plant
an unusual and fun addition
to arrangements. The tips of
the leaves turn bright red
with enough sunlight.

MATURE SIZE
18 inches
(45cm)

WATER
Average

SUN
Full sun,
light shade,
partial shade

HARDINESS
Zone 8b
15°F (−9.4°C)

PAIRS WITH
Aloe vera

Crassula perforata

STRING OF BUTTONS

Crassula perforata is a prolific plant and fun to add to arrangements. Like many succulents, it will get a tinge of red along the edges of its leaves with enough sunlight.

MATURE SIZE

18 inches
(45cm)

WATER

Average

SUN

Full sun,
partial shade

HARDINESS

Zone 9a
20°F (−6.6°C)

PAIRS WITH

Graptoveria
'Candle Blue'

Crassula rupestris

ROSARY VINE

This is another fun stacked succulent, but with two shades of green rather than red. It readily produces new branches and offsets.

MATURE SIZE

12 inches
(30cm)

WATER

Average

SUN

Full sun,
partial shade

HARDINESS

Zone 9b
25°F (−3.8°C)

PAIRS WITH

*Opuntia
microdasys albata*

Crassula 'Springtime'

When in bloom, the flowers on *Crassula* 'Springtime' attract birds and butterflies. It makes a great filler in container arrangements.

MATURE SIZE

18 inches (45cm)

WATER

Average

SUN

Full sun

HARDINESS

Zone 9a
20°F (−6.6°C)

PAIRS WITH

Aloe 'Christmas Carol'

Crassula
'Tom Thumb'

These little guys beautifully fill in the gaps between other succulents. They can also be a great backdrop for smaller rosette succulents.

MATURE SIZE
3 inches
(8cm)

WATER
Average

SUN
Full sun,
partial shade

HARDINESS
Zone 9b
25°F (−3.8°C)

PAIRS WITH
Aloe
'Doran Black'

Disocactus flagelliformis

RAT-TAIL CACTUS

As it grows longer, *Disocactus flagelliformis* will eventually bend and hang over the edge of the pot. It may even break, but it will continue growing downward after it falls. It is low maintenance and does well indoors.

MATURE SIZE

24 inches
(60cm)

WATER

Average

SUN

Full sun,
partial shade

HARDINESS

Zone 10a
30°F (−1.1°C)

PAIRS WITH

Echeveria elegans

Echeveria agavoides

LIPSTICK ECHEVERIA

This succulent grows well indoors and will maintain its deep color. However, to keep the "lipstick," this *Echeveria* will need full sun.

MATURE SIZE
6 inches
(15cm)

WATER
Average,
sensitive to
overwatering

SUN
Full sun,
light shade,
partial shade

HARDINESS
Zone 9a
20°F (−6.6°C)

PAIRS WITH
Echeveria
'Perle von
Nurnberg'

Echeveria
'Perle von Nurnberg'

'Perle von Nurnberg' is one of the most popular *Echeverias*. It has a unique, subtle color that works well in almost any arrangement.

MATURE SIZE
6 inches
(15cm)

WATER
Average

SUN
Full sun

HARDINESS
Zone 9b
20°F (−6.6°C)

PAIRS WITH
Senecio haworthii

Echeveria
'Black Prince'

The dark color of this *Echeveria* is very appealing. It does surprisingly well indoors, although it can easily lose its color without enough light.

MATURE SIZE
**6 inches
(15cm)**

WATER
Average

SUN
Full sun

HARDINESS
**Zone 9b
20°F (−6.6°C)**

PAIRS WITH
*Crassula
ovata*

Echeveria
'Doris Taylor'

WOOLY ROSE

This fuzzy succulent offsets easily, so you'll have an abundant collection quickly. It likes the shade, making it a great indoor plant.

MATURE SIZE

9 inches
(22cm)

WATER

Average

SUN

Light shade,
partial shade

HARDINESS

Zone 9b
20°F (−6.6°C)

PAIRS WITH

*Peperomia
graveolens*

Echeveria elegans

MEXICAN SNOWBALL

Echeveria elegans is frequently referred to as "hens and chicks." It offsets very easily and forms large clumps of rosettes. It needs really well-drained soil.

MATURE SIZE

6 inches
(15cm)

WATER

Average

SUN

Full sun,
partial shade

HARDINESS

Zone 9a
20°F (−6.6°C)

PAIRS WITH

*Portulacaria
afra*

Echeveria harmsii

This *Echeveria* tends to grow more bush-like rather than forming clumps of rosettes. It is quite popular due to its fuzzy texture and pink-tipped leaves.

MATURE SIZE

12 inches
(30cm)

WATER

Average

SUN

Full sun

HARDINESS

Zone 10b
35°F (1.7°C)

PAIRS WITH

Crassula
'Springtime'

Echeveria imbricata

This is one of the most popular *Echeverias*. It has a rich blue color, grows quickly, and clumps or produces offsets easily.

MATURE SIZE
6 inches (15cm)

WATER
Average

SUN
Full sun, partial shade

HARDINESS
Zone 9a 20°F (−6.6°C)

PAIRS WITH
Sedum morganianum

Echeveria 'Lola'

The pale color of *Echeveria* 'Lola' is quite unique. It provides subtle interest and contrast in arrangements.

MATURE SIZE

6 inches (15cm)

WATER

Average

SUN

Full sun, partial shade

HARDINESS

Zone 9b
25°F (−3.8°C)

PAIRS WITH

Gasteraloe 'Little Warty'

Echeveria purpusorum

This succulent looks quite tough or rough. It can change colors from green to brown to red depending on the amount of sunlight it gets.

MATURE SIZE
6 inches
(15cm)

WATER
Average

SUN
Full sun

HARDINESS
Zone 10a
30°F (−1.1°C)

PAIRS WITH
*Kalanchoe
longiflora
coccinea*

Echeveria runyonii 'Topsy Turvy'

'Topsy Turvy' is known for its unusual leaf shape. It offsets easily and provides great color interest in container arrangements.

MATURE SIZE

6 inches
(15cm)

WATER

Average,
sensitive to
overwatering

SUN

Full sun,
partial shade

HARDINESS

Zone 9b
25°F (−3.8°C)

PAIRS WITH

*Kalanchoe
tomentosa*

Euphorbia cereiformis

Euphorbia cereiformis produces offsets easily. The spines on this plant provide contrast to the bright green color. Take care when handling; its white sap can irritate skin on contact and is poisonous when ingested.

MATURE SIZE
18 inches
(45cm)

WATER
Average

SUN
Full sun,
partial shade

HARDINESS
Zone 10b
35°F (−1.7°C)

PAIRS WITH
*Crassula
marginalis rubra
variegata*

Euphorbia polygona 'Snowflake'

This striking black and white plant can grow straight or with a slight wave to its edges. Take care when handling; the white sap can irritate skin on contact and is poisonous when ingested.

MATURE SIZE

24 inches
(60cm)

WATER

Average

SUN

Full sun,
partial shade

HARDINESS

Zone 9a
20°F (−6.6°C)

PAIRS WITH

*Echeveria
agavoides*
'Lipstick'

Euphorbia tirucalli

STICKS OF FIRE

This *Euphorbia* creates a striking backdrop for landscapes or container arrangements. It turns bright red-orange in full sun. Like other *Euphorbias*, its white sap can irritate skin on contact and is poisonous when ingested.

MATURE SIZE
36 inches
(90cm)

WATER
Average

SUN
Full sun

HARDINESS
Zone 9a
20°F (−6.6°C)

PAIRS WITH
Echeveria imbricata

Faucaria tigrina

TIGER JAWS

The spines on this plant look intimidating, but are actually soft. With enough sunlight the leaves can turn purple. It readily produces offsets.

MATURE SIZE

3 inches (8cm)

WATER

Average

SUN

Full sun, partial shade

HARDINESS

Zone 9a
20°F (−6.6°C)

PAIRS WITH

Haworthia concolor

Fenestraria aurantiaca

BABY'S TOES

While many succulents form rosettes, this little plant produces translucent tubes. It grows quickly and does well indoors. With proper watering and sunlight it will bloom in late summer or early fall.

MATURE SIZE
3 inches
(8cm)

WATER
Average

SUN
Full sun,
light shade,
partial shade

HARDINESS
Zone 10a
30°F (−1.1°C)

PAIRS WITH
*Crassula
marnieriana*

Gasteraloe
'Little Warty'

The texture on this *Gastera-loe* makes you want to reach out and touch it. It is a sturdy plant that does well indoors.

MATURE SIZE

6 inches
(15cm)

WATER

Average

SUN

Full sun,
light shade,
partial shade

HARDINESS

Zone 9b
25°F (−3.8°C)

PAIRS WITH

Crassula rupestris

Gasteraloe
'Green Ice'

This succulent is a great
indoor grower. It offsets
easily and tolerates low light
as well as under-watering.

MATURE SIZE

12 inches
(30cm)

WATER

Average

SUN

Full sun,
light shade,
partial shade

HARDINESS

Zone 9b
25°F (−3.8°C)

PAIRS WITH

*Crassula
muscosa*

Graptosedum 'California Sunset'

Graptosedum 'California Sunset' is a great variety to use in arrangements. Its reddish hue contrasts nicely with the more common green succulents.

MATURE SIZE

12 inches (30cm)

WATER

Average

SUN

Full sun, partial shade

HARDINESS

Zone 10a
30°F (−1.1°C)

PAIRS WITH

Kalanchoe daigremontiana

Graptoveria
'Candle Blue'

One of the great things about this plant is that it maintains its color pretty well in shade. It puts off new offsets very quickly and forms small clumps.

MATURE SIZE

3 inches
(8cm)

WATER

Average

SUN

Full sun,
partial shade

HARDINESS

Zone 9b
25°F (−3.8°C)

PAIRS WITH

*Kalanchoe
pumila*

Graptoveria
'Fred Ives'

This *Graptoveria* is extremely easy to grow. It propagates from leaves and cuttings and also puts off new pups frequently. The color can vary from blue to red to green, depending on sunlight and temperature.

MATURE SIZE

18 inches
(45cm)

WATER

Average

SUN

Full sun,
partial shade

HARDINESS

Zone 9b
25°F (−3.8°C)

PAIRS WITH

Crassula ovata
'Gollum'

Graptoveria
'Silver Star'

The tips of this *Graptoveria* come to a narrow point, more so than most *Echeverias* or *Graptoverias*, which gives it an unusual look. It is also more cold tolerant than most in this family.

MATURE SIZE

3 inches
(8cm)

WATER

Average

SUN

Full sun,
light shade,
partial shade

HARDINESS

Zone 7b
5°F (−14.9°C)

PAIRS WITH

*Haworthia
coarctata*

Gymnocalycium mihanovichii

MOON CACTUS

These ornamental cacti are quite popular house-plants. They are easy to take care of and come in a variety of colors. The most common color is red.

MATURE SIZE

12 inches
(30cm)

WATER

Average

SUN

Light shade

HARDINESS

Zone 9b
25°F (−3.8°C)

PAIRS WITH

*Kalanchoe
humilis*

Haworthia coarctata

Haworthia coarctata forms tight clusters and produces offsets easily. It can turn pink in the cold or with enough sunlight.

MATURE SIZE
12 inches
(30cm)

WATER
Average

SUN
Full sun,
partial shade

HARDINESS
Zone 9b
25°F (−3.8°C)

PAIRS WITH
*Echeveria
purpusorum*

Haworthia concolor

This *Haworthia* has some subtle details in texture that make it quite stunning. It grows well indoors because it tolerates low-light environments.

MATURE SIZE
6 inches
(15cm)

WATER
Average

SUN
Full sun,
partial shade

HARDINESS
Zone 9a
20°F (−6.6°C)

PAIRS WITH
Gasteraloe
'Green Ice'

Haworthia fasciata

ZEBRA PLANT

The Zebra Plant is one of the most popular plants in the *Haworthia* genus. Its green leaves with white stripes and pointed tips are striking in arrangements. It is also one of the best indoor succulents because it tolerates low light well and doesn't require much water.

MATURE SIZE

6 inches
(15cm)

WATER

Average

SUN

Full sun,
light shade,
partial shade

HARDINESS
Zone 9b
25°F (−3.8°C)

PAIRS WITH

*Kalanchoe
tomentosa*

Haworthia reinwardtii

Haworthia reinwardtii clumps easily and creates tight and compact pointed forms. It does very well in low light and is slow to rot from overwatering.

MATURE SIZE

12 inches
(30cm)

WATER

Average

SUN

Partial shade

HARDINESS

Zone 11
40°F (4.5°C)

PAIRS WITH

Gymnocalycium mihanovichii

Haworthia retusa

STAR CACTUS

This plant absorbs light through its translucent skin. It does very well indoors in low-light environments.

MATURE SIZE
3 inches
(8cm)

WATER
Average

SUN
Full sun,
light shade,
partial shade

HARDINESS
Zone 9b
25°F (−3.8°C)

PAIRS WITH
Crassula capitella
'Campfire'

Kalanchoe daigremontiana

MOTHER OF THOUSANDS

For some, this plant can seem like a noxious weed as it propagates extremely easily from bulbils growing along the edges of its leaves. For others, it's fun to grow in containers and watch the plants multiply.

MATURE SIZE

36 inches
(90cm)

WATER

Above
average

SUN

Full sun,
partial shade

HARDINESS

Zone 9b
25°F (−3.8°C)

PAIRS WITH

Graptoveria
'Fred Ives'

Kalanchoe luciae

PADDLE PLANT

With enough sunlight or in colder weather, the "paddles" on this succulent turn a deep red. It provides a nice backdrop for other succulents in an arrangement.

MATURE SIZE
24 inches
(60cm)

WATER
Average

SUN
Full sun,
light shade,
partial shade

HARDINESS
Zone 9a
20°F (−6.6°C)

PAIRS WITH
Aloe
'Doran Black'

Kalanchoe humilis

The red and green variegation on this succulent draws attention when placed with other succulents. It tolerates neglect well, so it's a great beginner plant. It generally blooms in midsummer.

MATURE SIZE

6 inches (15cm)

WATER

Average

SUN

Full sun, light shade, partial shade

HARDINESS

Zone 8a 10°F (−12.2°C)

PAIRS WITH

Senecio radicans

Kalanchoe longiflora coccinea

While this succulent can look good alone, it also makes a great filler plant in arrangements. It maintains its red color best in full sun.

MATURE SIZE

48 inches
(120cm)

WATER

Average

SUN

Full sun

HARDINESS

Zone 10a
30°F (−1.1°C)

PAIRS WITH

*Aloe
brevifolia*

Kalanchoe marnieriana

This thin-leafed succulent propagates easily from its leaves and cuttings. It provides a nice filler and unique shape in arrangements.

MATURE SIZE

18 inches
(45cm)

WATER

Average

SUN

Full sun,
partial shade

HARDINESS

Zone 11
40°F (4.5°C)

PAIRS WITH

Graptoveria
'Fred Ives'

Kalanchoe pumila

FLOWER DUST PLANT

The dusty grey of *Kalanchoe pumila* adds a subtle accent to a succulent arrangement. It gets bright pink flowers in early spring.

MATURE SIZE
12 inches
(30cm)

WATER
Above
average

SUN
Full sun,
partial shade

HARDINESS
Zone 10a
30°F (−1.1°C)

PAIRS WITH
*Sedum
clavatum*

Kalanchoe tomentosa

PANDA PLANT, CHOCOLATE SOLDIER

Kalanchoe tomentosa is a very common succulent and fairly easy to grow. It comes in two main colors: a grayish blue (Panda Plant) and golden brown (Chocolate Soldier).

MATURE SIZE

24 inches
(60cm)

WATER

Average

SUN

Full sun,
partial shade

HARDINESS

Zone 9b
25°F (−3.8°C)

PAIRS WITH

Aeonium 'Kiwi'

Lithops

LIVING STONES

Lithops come in a variety of colors, some of which can be quite expensive. They do not like to be watered very frequently and will die quickly from overwatering.

MATURE SIZE

1 inch
(3cm)

WATER

Below
average

SUN

Full sun,
light shade,
partial shade

HARDINESS

Zone 10a
30°F (−1.1°C)

PAIRS WITH

*Pleiospilos
nelii*

Mammillaria elongata

LADYFINGER CACTUS

Mammillaria elongata is a small clumping cactus. It is easy to grow and propagate, so it's great for beginners.

MATURE SIZE

3 inches
(8cm)

WATER

Average

SUN

Full sun

HARDINESS

Zone 9b
25°F (-3.8°C)

PAIRS WITH

Sedum adolphii

Mammillaria gracilis fragilis

This cactus can add a lot of visual interest to an arrangement. It offsets quickly, grows well indoors, and is easy to take care of.

MATURE SIZE

3 inches
(8cm)

WATER

Average

SUN

Full sun,
partial shade,
light shade

HARDINESS

Zone 9b
25°F (-3.8°C)

PAIRS WITH

*Senecio
barbertonicus*

Mammillaria plumosa

FEATHER CACTUS

Don't be deceived by the soft, fuzzy look of this cactus. It does have spines that quickly stick in your fingers. It generally blooms in spring and has white flowers.

MATURE SIZE

3 inches
(8cm)

WATER

Average

SUN

Full sun,
partial shade

HARDINESS

Zone 9a
20°F (-6.6°C)

PAIRS WITH

*Crassula
muscosa*

Mammillaria rhodantha

RAINBOW PINCUSHION

When in full bloom, this cactus has a ring of bright pink flowers around the top. It is an easy-to-grow cactus and does well indoors.

MATURE SIZE
12 inches
(30cm)

WATER
Average

SUN
Full sun,
light shade,
partial shade

HARDINESS
Zone 9a
20°F (-6.6°C)

PAIRS WITH
Ceropegia woodii variegata

Opuntia microdasys albata

ANGEL WINGS, BUNNY EARS

This cactus looks cute and fuzzy, but the spines stick easily in fingers and are difficult to remove. Its spines are generally one of two colors: white (Angel Wings) or yellow (Bunny Ears).

MATURE SIZE

12 inches
(30cm)

WATER

Average

SUN

Full sun,
light shade,
partial shade

HARDINESS

Zone 9b
25°F (-3.8°C)

PAIRS WITH

Echeveria
'Lola'

Oreocereus celsianus

OLD MAN OF THE ANDES

Although it is quite hairy, it's easy to see the spines on this cactus. It does well in containers, but can grow up to 10 feet (3m) in the ground.

MATURE SIZE

10 feet
(3m)

WATER

Average

SUN

Full sun,
partial shade

HARDINESS

Zone 8a
10°F (-12.2°C)

PAIRS WITH

*Faucaria
tigrina*

Pachyveria glauca 'Little Jewel'

This is a stiff-leaved clumping succulent. It can tolerate a variety of growing environments, including too much or too little water and sunlight.

MATURE SIZE
3 inches
(8cm)

WATER
Average

SUN
Full sun,
partial shade

HARDINESS
Zone 10a
30°F (−1.1°C)

PAIRS WITH
Echeveria runyonii
'Topsy Turvy'

Peperomia graveolens

This succulent works well as a filler in container arrangements. It is a little bit delicate to handle, but does well once it's rooted in its container.

MATURE SIZE
12 inches
(30cm)

WATER
Average

SUN
Light shade,
partial shade

HARDINESS
Zone 10a
30°F (−1.1°C)

PAIRS WITH
Graptoveria
'Silver Star'

Pleiospilos nelii

SPLITROCK, MIMICRY PLANT

While similar to the *Lithops* varieties in their needs for water and light, *Pleiospilos nelii* have a different shape and almost always have another section of plant growing in the middle of the lower leaves. They do not tolerate overwatering.

MATURE SIZE
3 inches
(8cm)

WATER
Average,
sensitive to
overwatering

SUN
Full sun,
light shade,
partial shade

HARDINESS
Zone 9b
25°F (−3.8°C)

PAIRS WITH
Lithops

Portulacaria afra

ELEPHANT BUSH

This is a very popular succulent that does well in the ground as well as in containers. The variegated variety is also quite popular. Both varieties make great plants for bonsai.

MATURE SIZE
6 feet
(1.8m)

WATER
Average

SUN
Full sun

HARDINESS
Zone 9a
20°F (−6.6°C)

PAIRS WITH
Graptosedum
'California Sunset'

Rhipsalis cereuscula

CORAL CACTUS

This narrow-leaved cactus has soft spines that don't tend to stick to fingers. It propagates easily from cuttings. The branches create interesting shapes that resemble coral.

MATURE SIZE

24 inches (60cm)

WATER

Average

SUN

Light shade, partial shade, full shade

HARDINESS

Zone 10a

30°F (−1.1°C)

PAIRS WITH

Haworthia retusa

Rhipsalis ewaldiana

In colder temperatures or with enough sunlight, the tips of this succulent will turn slightly orange or yellow. It grows very well indoors with low lighting.

MATURE SIZE
24 inches
(60cm)

WATER
Average

SUN
Light shade,
partial shade,
full shade

HARDINESS
Zone 10a
30°F (-1.1°C)

PAIRS WITH
Aloe
'Twilight Zone'

Sansevieria trifasciata

SNAKE PLANT, MOTHER-IN-LAW'S TONGUE

This is a very common house plant. It has many cultivars, which have a variety of patterns on their leaves. It does very well in low lighting.

MATURE SIZE
48 inches
(120cm)

WATER
Average

SUN
Light shade

HARDINESS
Zone 10a
30°F (−1.1°C)

PAIRS WITH
Rhipsalis cereuscula

Schlumbergera truncata

THANKSGIVING CACTUS, CHRISTMAS CACTUS

As you may guess, this plant is frequently purchased around Thanksgiving or Christmas time, which is when it normally blooms. There are several varieties with different flower colors including pink, red and white, and sometimes even orange and yellow.

MATURE SIZE
12 inches
(30cm)

WATER
Average

SUN
Light shade

HARDINESS
Zone 10b
35°F (1.7°C)

PAIRS WITH
Sansevieria trifasciata

Sedum adolphii

GOLDEN SEDUM

This clumping *Sedum* is great for succulent projects and arrangements. It grows very well from cuttings and is easy to take care of.

MATURE SIZE

12 inches
(30cm)

WATER

Average

SUN

Full sun

HARDINESS

Zone 9a
20°F (−6.6°C)

PAIRS WITH

*Crassula arbores-
cens undulatifolia*

Sedum clavatum

This succulent forms small stems with lots of rosettes. It can get a hint of pink on the edge of its leaves with enough sunlight.

MATURE SIZE
6 inches
(15cm)

WATER
Average

SUN
Full sun,
partial shade

HARDINESS
Zone 9a
20°F (–6.6°C)

PAIRS WITH
*Aloe
haworthioides*

Sedum morganianum

DONKEY'S TAIL, BURRO TAIL

Burro Tail is one of the most popular succulents. It's easy to grow and to propagate. It is quite a sight when fully grown in strands about 4 feet (1.2m) long!

MATURE SIZE

48 inches (120cm)

WATER

Average

SUN

Full sun, light shade, partial shade

HARDINESS

Zone 10b 35°F (1.7°C)

PAIRS WITH

Aloe 'Black Beauty'

Sedum nussbaumerianum
'Orange Delight'

Often mistaken for *Sedum adolphii*, *Sedum nussbaumerianum* has a beautiful orange color when it receives enough sunlight. It clumps easily and grows well from cuttings.

MATURE SIZE
12 inches
(30cm)

WATER
Average

SUN
Full sun

HARDINESS
Zone 9b
25°F (−3.8°C)

PAIRS WITH
Mammillaria gracilis fragilis

Sedum pachyphyllum

JELLY BEANS

This is a popular succulent because it has unique coloring and is easy to grow. It also propagates well from leaves and cuttings.

MATURE SIZE
12 inches
(30cm)

WATER
Average

SUN
Full sun

HARDINESS
Zone 8b
15°F (−9.4°C)

PAIRS WITH
Crassula arborescens

Sedum praealtum

SHRUBBY STONECROP

This succulent has some similarities to *Crassula ovata*, but its leaves form rosettes. It is one of the more hardy *Sedums* and can tolerate some frost and extended cold weather.

MATURE SIZE
12 inches
(30cm)

WATER
Average

SUN
Full sun,
partial shade

HARDINESS
Zone 7a
0°F (−17.7°C)

PAIRS WITH
Crassula
'Springtime'

Sedum rubrotinctum

PORK AND BEANS

This is a very popular succulent. With plenty of sunlight, it gets a deep red hue on the end of the leaves. When leaves fall off, they easily take root and form new plants.

MATURE SIZE

12 inches
(30cm)

WATER

Average

SUN

Full sun

HARDINESS

Zone 9a
20°F (−6.6°C)

PAIRS WITH

*Oreocereus
celsianus*

Sedum rupestre

SPRUCE-LEAVED STONECROP

This succulent makes a great "filler" and even "spiller" in arrangements. It tolerates cold very well and can survive under snow over the winter.

MATURE SIZE
6 inches
(15cm)

WATER
Average

SUN
Full sun,
partial shade

HARDINESS
Zone 4a
−30°F (−34.4°C)

PAIRS WITH
Sempervivum
'Pacific Devil's Food'

Sempervivum arachnoideum

COBWEB HOUSELEEK

Like most *Sempervivums*, this succulent offsets very easily and can multiply significantly in just a few months. It does very well in cold weather, but is also happy in warmer climates.

MATURE SIZE

3 inches
(8cm)

WATER

Average

SUN

Full sun

HARDINESS

Zone 5a
−20°F (−28.8°C)

PAIRS WITH

*Sedum
rupestre*

Sempervivum 'Pacific Devil's Food'

HEN AND CHICKS

The dark purple coloring of this succulent makes a stunning addition to a container arrangement. Its darkest purple will show in cold weather or with plenty of sunlight.

MATURE SIZE

3 inches
(8cm)

WATER

Average

SUN

Full sun

HARDINESS

Zone 4a
−30°F (−34.4°C)

PAIRS WITH

Sempervivum arachnoideum

Senecio haworthii

COCOON PLANT

This succulent can be hard to find, but it makes a great addition to any collection. With its fuzzy texture and white coloring, it really stands out in an arrangement.

MATURE SIZE
6 inches
(15cm)

WATER
Average

SUN
Full sun

HARDINESS
Zone 9b
25°F (−3.8°C)

PAIRS WITH
*Senecio
barbertonicus*

Senecio barbertonicus

Senecio barbertonicus is a great "filler" or "thriller" plant, depending on the height of your arrangement. Its bright green color will brighten up a container of succulents with more subtle tones.

MATURE SIZE
6 feet
(1.8m)

WATER
Average,
sensitive to
overwatering

SUN
Full sun,
light shade,
partial shade

HARDINESS
Zone 9b
25°F (−3.8°C)

PAIRS WITH
Mammillaria rhodantha

Senecio mandraliscae

BLUE CHALK STICKS

Blue Chalk Sticks is a very popular succulent and is frequently used as a ground-cover. It also adds a unique blue color to container arrangements.

MATURE SIZE
18 inches
(45cm)

WATER
Average

SUN
Full sun

HARDINESS
Zone 10a
30°F (−1.1°C)

PAIRS WITH
Echeveria
'Perle von Nurnberg'

Senecio radicans

STRING OF BANANAS

This succulent is good for hanging baskets. It makes a great "spiller" plant in container arrangements and pairs well with many other succulents.

MATURE SIZE

24 inches
(60cm)

WATER

Average

SUN

Light shade

HARDINESS

Zone 10a
30°F (−1.1°C)

PAIRS WITH

Echeveria
'Doris Taylor'

Senecio rowleyanus

STRING OF PEARLS

String of Pearls is one of the most well-known and common succulents. It is especially stunning when it reaches 2 feet (.5m) in length (and sometimes it grows even longer).

MATURE SIZE
24 inches
(60cm)

WATER
Average

SUN
Light shade

HARDINESS
Zone 8a
10°F (−12.2°C)

PAIRS WITH
Echeveria
'Doris Taylor'

Senecio vitalis

NARROW-LEAF CHALK STICKS

Simliar to *Senecio barbertonicus* except blue-green in color, this succulent is great in containers. It easily fills in the gaps between other succulents while adding visual interest and texture.

MATURE SIZE
24 inches
(60cm)

WATER
Average

SUN
Full sun

HARDINESS
Zone 9b
25°F (−3.8°C)

PAIRS WITH
Pachyveria glauca

APPENDIX A: INDEX BY COLOR

BLUE-GREEN

Aloe brevifolia

Crassula arborescens

Crassula falcata

Echeveria elegans

Echeveria imbricata

Echeveria runyonii 'Topsy Turvy'

Fenestraria aurantiaca

Gasteraloe 'Green Ice'

Graptoveria 'Candle Blue'

Kalanchoe tomentosa

Pachyveria glauca 'Little Jewel'

Sedum clavatum

Sedum morganianum

Sedum pachyphyllum

Sedum rupestre

Senecio mandraliscae

Senecio vitalis

BROWN

Kalanchoe tomentosa

Lithops

Mammillaria elongata

GREEN

Adromischus cristatus

Aloe haworthioides

Aloe juvenna

Aloe nobilis

Aloe
'Twilight Zone'

Aloe vera

Cereus bildmannianus uruguayanus

Cotyledon tomentosa ladismithensis

Crassula arborescens undulatifolia

Crassula muscosa

Crassula ovata

Crassula rupestris

Crassula 'Springtime'

Disocactus flagelliformis

Echeveria 'Doris Taylor'

Euphorbia cereiformis

Gasteraloe 'Little Warty'

Graptoveria 'Silver Star'

Haworthia coarctata

Haworthia concolor

Haworthia fasciata

Haworthia reinwardtii

Haworthia retusa

Kalanchoe daigremontiana

Kalanchoe marnieriana

Mammillaria rhodantha

Portulacaria afra

Rhipsalis cereuscula

Rhipsalis ewaldiana

Sansevieria trifasciata

Schlumbergera truncata

Sempervivum arachnoideum

GREEN

Senecio barbertonicus

Senecio radicans

Senecio rowleyanus

GREEN WITH ORANGE

Aloe 'Christmas Carol'

Crassula ovata 'Gollum'

Euphorbia tirucalli

GREEN WITH PINK OR RED

Aloe 'Crosby's Prolific'

Anacampseros telephiastrum variegata

Echeveria harmsii

Crassula capitella 'Campfire'

Crassula marnieriana

Crassula perforata

Crassula 'Tom Thumb'

Echeveria agavoides

Gymnocalycium mihanovichii

Kalanchoe luciae

Sedum praealtum

Sedum rubrotinctum

GREEN WITH PURPLE

Adromischus maculatus

Anacampseros rufescens

Faucaria tigrina

Kalanchoe humilis

GREEN WITH YELLOW AND PINK

Aeonium 'Kiwi'

Aeonium 'Sunburst'

Crassula marginalis rubra variegata

GRAY

Kalanchoe pumila   *Pleiospilos nelii*

ORANGE

Sedum adolphii   *Sedum nussbaumerianum*
'Orange Delight'

PINK

Ceropegia woodii
variegata   *Graptoveria*
'Fred Ives'

PURPLE

Aeonium arboreum
'Zwartkop'   *Aloe*
'Black Beauty'   *Echeveria*
'Perle von Nurnberg'   *Echeveria*
'Black Prince'   *Echeveria*
purpusorum   *Sempervivum*
'Pacific Devil's Food'

RED

Graptosedum
'California Sunset'   *Kalanchoe longiflora*
coccinea

WHITE

Aloe
'Doran Black'   *Cephalocereus*
senilis   *Echeveria*
'Lola'   *Euphorbia polygona*
'Snowflake'   *Mammillaria*
gracilis fragilis

Peperomia
graveolens   *Mammillaria*
plumosa   *Opuntia microdasys*
albata   *Oreocereus celsianus*   *Senecio haworthii*

APPENDIX B: INDEX BY HEIGHT

TRAILING SUCCULENTS

Senecio radicans
(24 inches long; 60cm)

Senecio rowleyanus
(24 inches long; 60cm)

Ceropegia woodii variegata
(36 inches long; 90cm)

Sedum morganianum
(48 inches long; 120cm)

NON-TRAILING SUCCULENTS

Lithops
(1 inch; 2.5cm)

Anacampseros rufescens
(3 inches; 8cm)

*Anacampseros
telephiastrum variegata*
(3 inches; 8cm)

Crassula
'Tom Thumb'
(3 inches; 8cm)

Faucaria tigrina
(3 inches; 8cm)

Fenestraria aurantiaca
(3 inches; 8cm)

Graptoveria
'Candle Blue'
(3 inches; 8cm)

Graptoveria
'Silver Star'
(3 inches; 8cm)

Haworthia retusa
(3 inches; 8cm)

Mammillaria elongata
(3 inches; 8cm)

*Mammillaria
gracilis fragilis*
(3 inches; 8cm)

Mammillaria plumosa
(3 inches; 8cm)

Pachyveria glauca
'Little Jewel'
(3 inches; 8cm)

Pleiospilos nelii
(3 inches; 8cm)

*Sempervivum
arachnoideum*
(3 inches; 8cm)

Sempervivum
'Pacific Devil's Food'
(3 inches; 8cm)

Adromischus maculatus
(6 inches; 15cm)

Aloe brevifolia
(6 inches; 15cm)

Aloe
'Christmas Carol'
(6 inches; 15cm)

Aloe
'Crosby's Prolific'
(6 inches; 15cm)

Aloe
'Doran Black'
(6 inches; 15cm)

*Crassula marginalis
rubra variegata*
(6 inches; 15cm)

Crassula marnieriana
(6 inches; 15cm)

Echeveria agavoides
(6 inches; 15cm)

Echeveria
'Perle von Nurnberg'
(6 inches; 15cm)

Echeveria
'Black Prince'
(6 inches; 15cm)

Echeveria elegans
(6 inches; 15cm)

Echeveria imbricata
(6 inches; 15cm)

Echeveria
'Lola'
(6 inches; 15cm)

Echeveria purpusorum
(6 inches; 15cm)

Echeveria runyonii
'Topsy Turvy'
(6 inches; 15cm)

Gasteraloe
'Little Warty'
(6 inches; 15cm)

Haworthia concolor
(6 inches; 15cm)

Haworthia fasciata
(6 inches; 15cm)

Kalanchoe humilis
(6 inches; 15cm)

Sedum clavatum
(6 inches; 15cm)

Sedum rupestre
(6 inches; 15cm)

Senecio haworthii
(6 inches; 15cm)

Echeveria
'Doris Taylor'
(9 inches; 22cm)

Aeonium
'Kiwi'
(12 inches; 30cm)

Aloe
'Black Beauty'
(12 inches; 30cm)

Aloe haworthioides
(12 inches; 30cm)

Aloe nobilis
(12 inches; 30cm)

Aloe
'Twilight Zone'
(12 inches; 30cm)

*Cotyledon tomentosa
ladismithensis*
(12 inches; 30cm)

Crassula capitella
'Campfire'
(12 inches; 30cm)

Crassula muscosa
(12 inches; 30cm)

Crassula rupestris
(12 inches; 30cm)

Echeveria harmsii
(12 inches; 30cm)

Gasteraloe
'Green Ice'
(12 inches; 30cm)

Graptosedum
'California Sunset'
(12 inches; 30cm)

Gymnocalycium mihanovichii
(12 inches; 30cm)

Haworthia coarctata
(12 inches; 30cm)

Haworthia reinwardtii
(12 inches; 30cm)

Kalanchoe marnieriana
(12 inches; 30cm)

Kalanchoe pumila
(12 inches; 30cm)

Mammillaria rhodantha
(12 inches; 30cm)

Opuntia microdasys albata
(12 inches; 30cm)

Peperomia graveolens
(12 inches; 30cm)

Schlumbergera truncata
(12 inches; 30cm)

Sedum adolphii
(12 inches; 30cm)

Sedum nussbaumerianum 'Orange Delight'
(12 inches; 30cm)

Sedum pachyphyllum
(12 inches; 30cm)

Sedum praealtum
(12 inches; 30cm)

Sedum rubrotinctum
(12 inches; 30cm)

Adromischus cristatus
(18 inches; 45cm)

Aeonium
'Sunburst'
(18 inches; 45cm)

Crassula falcata
(18 inches; 45cm)

Crassula ovata
'Gollum'
(18 inches; 45cm)

Crassula perforata
(18 inches; 45cm)

Crassula
'Springtime'
(18 inches; 45cm)

Euphorbia cereiformis
(18 inches; 45cm)

Graptoveria
'Fred Ives'
(18 inches; 45cm)

Senecio mandraliscae
(18 inches; 45cm)

Aloe juvenna
(24 inches; 60cm)

Aloe vera
(24 inches; 60cm)

Disocactus flagelliformis
(24 inches; 60cm)

Euphorbia polygona
'Snowflake'
(24 inches; 60cm)

Kalanchoe luciae
(24 inches; 60cm)

Kalanchoe tomentosa
(24 inches; 60cm)

Rhipsalis cereuscula
(24 inches; 60cm)

Rhipsalis ewaldiana
(24 inches; 60cm)

Senecio vitalis
(24 inches; 60cm)

*Cereus hildmannianus
uruguayanus*
(36 inches; 90cm)

*Crassula arborescens
undulatifolia*
(36 inches; 90cm)

Euphorbia tirucalli
(36 inches; 90cm)

*Kalanchoe
daigremontiana*
(36 inches; 90cm)

*Aeonium arboreum
'Zwartkop'*
(48 inches; 120cm)

*Kalanchoe
longiflora coccinea*
(48 inches; 120cm)

Sansevieria trifasciata
(48 inches; 120cm)

Crassula arborescens
(6 feet; 1.8m)

Crassula ovata
(6 feet; 1.8m)

Portulacaria afra
(6 feet; 1.8m)

Senecio barbertonicus
(6 feet; 1.8m)

Oreocereus celsianus
(10 feet; 3m)

Cephalocereus senilis
(40 feet; 12m)

GLOSSARY

analogous colors   Two or three colors that are next to each other on the color wheel, such as green, blue, and purple or green, blue-green, and blue.

bulbil   The place on the outside edge of a succulent leaf where a new plant may form.

callous   When the end of a plant heals by drying out and hardening.

chick   A new plant with roots produced by the main plant. Also called a pup, baby, or offset.

coconut coir   A fiber taken from coconut husks. It can be used with diatomaceous earth to create a well-draining soil.

complementary colors   Two colors that are opposite each other on a color wheel, such as blue and orange.

cutting   A section of plant that has been removed from the main section. Cuttings do not have roots but will grow new roots eventually.

diamond-tip drill bit   A drill bit that is hollow and circular with granules of diamond on the end, allowing it to bore into a variety of harder materials, such as glass.

diatomaceous earth   A porous sedimentary rock that absorbs water. It works well in combination with coconut coir for creating a well-draining succulent soil. It can also be used by itself as soil where more drainage is needed.

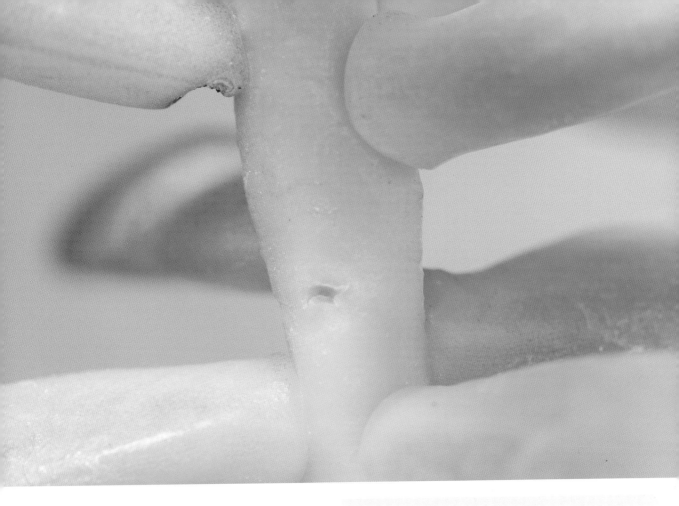

direct sunlight   Sunlight that falls directly on a plant.

dormancy   The period of time in which a succulent stops growing or grows very little.

drainage hole   A hole in the bottom of the pot that allows excess water to flow out of the pot.

filler   A succulent that is used in an arrangement to fill in the gaps between the main focal point and the succulents spilling over the edge.

grow light   An artificial light used for indoor plants. Grow lights provide the correct color spectrum of light that plants need to grow.

indirect sunlight   Bright, diffused light in which no sunlight falls directly on a plant.

leaf node   The area on the stem of a succulent where a leaf was once attached.

leggy   Used to describe a plant that has become elongated with excess space between the leaves, generally caused by insufficient sunlight.

mealybugs   Small bugs often found on succulents that suck the sap out of the leaves. They are coated with a white cobweb-like substance that has characteristics of wax.

monochromatic colors   Various tints and shades of the same color.

peat moss An absorbent moss generally used in potting soil.

perlite A volcanic glass that expands when in contact with water.

plug An individual succulent that has roots. This could have been a cutting previously or a chick removed from the main plant.

propagate Creating new plants from cuttings, leaves, chicks, and seeds.

pumice A light and porous volcanic rock.

root bound When a potted succulent's roots fill the entire container and become tightly compacted.

rot Blackening and/or softening of the stem or leaves of a succulent caused by overwatering.

scar Damage on the leaf of a succulent.

spiller A succulent that hangs over the edge of the pot in an arrangement.

spine A needle-like projection on a succulent or cactus that acts as a defense for the plant. These can vary from long and stiff to small and hair-like.

succulent   A plant that stores water in its leaves, stem, or roots.

sunburn   Dark spots on the leaves of a succulent caused by too much direct sun exposure. Extreme sunburn will bleach the plant leaves, which will turn them light brown.

temporary arrangement   An arrangement created without any soil that is not likely to last for more than a few days without being repotted.

thriller   Generally a tall or spikey succulent used as the main focal point in a succulent arrangement.

top dressing   Rocks or other materials used to cover the soil. They help prevent the soil from moving when watered and can add visual interest to an arrangement.

topiary   A moss form used to create unique shapes for planting.

watering stone   A stone placed in an arrangement to pour water on, allowing the arrangement to be watered evenly without disturbing the plants or soil.

well-draining soil   A soil type that allows water to flow through easily and does not hold water or stay soggy for very long.

RESOURCES

While the internet is full of information about growing and purchasing succulents, it can be hard to know which sources are reputable. The following sources for purchasing succulents are well established and provide high-quality plants. The informational sources will help you with various aspects of growing succulents, whether it's plant identification, growing indoors, growing outdoors, or just finding information about a specific succulent. For beautiful pottery, you'll love the shops listed here as well. If you're looking for inspiring photos of succulents, be sure to check out the resources in the inspiration section for an overload of gorgeous succulents!

ONLINE SUCCULENT STORES

Altman Plants

altmanplants.com/plant-shop

A large selection of succulents, including a few rare species.

The Succulent Perch

thesucculentperch.com

Succulent rooftop birdhouses, wreaths, design kits, and information about succulent care.

Mountain Crest Gardens

mountaincrestgardens.com

Wide variety of succulents for sale, with an especially large selection of cold-hardy succulents.

I Dream of Succulents

etsy.com/shop/iDreamOfSucculents

Various container arrangements and some individual plants.

Succulent Gardens

sgplants.com

Letter planters and living pictures. A great place to buy shadowbox frames for living pictures.

Succulent Central

succulentcentral.com

A variety of bare-root and potted succulents as well as cuttings.

INFORMATION ABOUT SUCCULENTS

Waterwise Botanicals

waterwisebotanicals.com

Find out more about individual plants as well as landscaping with succulents.

Dave's Garden

davesgarden.com

Information about most plants, including succulents. General growing information as well as plant-specific information.

Succulents and Sunshine

succulentsandsunshine.com

Guide for growing succulents and projects you can create with succulents.

The Cactus and Succulent Plant Mall

cactus-mall.com

Find succulent societies, local nurseries, and online succulent stores.

Sweetstuff's Sassy Succulents

sweetstuffssassysucculents.com

Fun photos and articles about succulent gardens.

Design with Diversity

laurabalaoro.com

Great tips for growing succulents and garden inspiration.

Design for Serenity

designforserenity.com

Succulent garden design tips and inspiration.

INSPIRATION

Santa Barbara Succulent Art
facebook.com/sbsucculentart

Succulent arrangements for weddings and events.

Redeeming Eden
facebook.com/RedeemingEden

A variety of arrangements perfect for home décor.

Succulove
instagram.com/succulove

A collection of images of succulents in containers and gardens throughout the world.

Succulent Café
succulentcafeoceanside.com

An amazing café filled with beautiful succulent creations.

Dalla Vita
dallavita.com

Succulent arrangements perfect for growing at home.

POTTERY AND CONTAINERS

Susan Aach
susanaachceramics.com

High-fired, hand-built pottery perfect for filling with succulents.

Hedge
hedgeoutdoor.com

Colorful hanging planters with a modern design.

Donna Taylor Pottery
succulent-pottery.com

Handcrafted pottery in small sizes, great for growing succulents indoors.

INDEX

H

I-J-K

L-M

N-O

S